LIMINAL
LIFE

NAVIGATING TRANSITIONS WITH AUTHENTICITY

CA JALONEN

ISBN: 979-8-9900063-0-0

Imprint: Liminality Library

Editors: Darlene Turriff and Nicole Washburn

Cover Design: Robert Williams, ilovemycover.com

Book Layout: Robert Williams

Photography Credit: Carrie Jalonen

To order more copies or find out about other programs, visit www.cajalonen.com

for Kim

This work was created on the ancestral lands of the Skokomish and Suquamish tribes with acknowledgement of their continued presence and active role they play in the local communities of Kitsap.

CONTENTS

THE GLOAMING

I step over the threshold out into the cool of twilight. It is getting late - the sun has already sunken low and taken all the golden shafts of light with it. All that is left is a purple-blue hue that tints everything in shadow. The thrush and the juncos have finally settled into their nests and the night creatures aren't stirring yet.

It is markedly quiet and still.

The evergreens towards the west overlay the last faint glow of yellow in the sky. They are silhouetted so sharply it looks like they've been drawn by a great big etch-a-sketch.

The air is taking on a cool tang that wasn't there earlier in the afternoon heat. It smells fresh and plantlike. A bit *moist*, if you can handle the word.

Out of the corner of my eye I spy a squirrel sitting lumped up in the planter bed off the end of the patio and I wonder why he hasn't scurried away to cozy up for the night. I don't really like the way he's looking at me.

"*Shoo!*" I whisper.

Nothing. Curious and a bit cheeky! I take a step towards him, thinking it would startle him into running. Nothing. How odd.

Peering harder into the shadows and slowly walking forward, I realize with a giggle and a grin - it is a gnome. Not the kind that has crossed from his world into this one because it is the time-between-times. Just your garden variety, well... garden gnome. All resin and chipped paint with a tubby tummy, grinning back at me. *Imp*.

Ahh, the mysteries of the gloaming...

INTRODUCTION - THRESHOLDS

Limin: /n/ threshold
Liminal: /adj/ The feeling of betweenness in a transitional time
Liminality: /abstract n/ state of discomfort or unease caused by ambiguity

The gloaming.

I love the word. Say it out loud. It feels so good in the mouth. *Gloaming.* It is one of those words that sounds like the thing it is describing. It has an almost sad sound to it. It is the perfect word to describe what is otherwise called evening or twilight. Yet another gift of the Scottish people to language.

There are wonderful, imaginative stories and ideas around this time of day - this gloaming. In fantasy fiction, this time of day is when the veil between our world - the world of man - and the world of the fae or the fairies is thinned and can be traversed. Oooooh! *Magic!* Little creatures of fantasy, some good, some… not so good, come to play in our world. To dance within stone circles under the stars or sour the milk.

The gloaming was the first thing I realized I had a connection with as I began to awaken to this concept of liminality. It is an in-between time. A "middle mystery." A time when it seems *anything* could happen. And *anything* is awfully big. *Anything* can feel - scary.

I learned the word liminal in early 2021. I was explaining to a therapist one day my feeling of discomfort of living with my hands open: holding two seemingly opposing thoughts - the Both/And concept. I was beginning to recognize many things as being this way. Times of day, physical spaces, and feelings-uncomfortable feelings. In truth… all of *Life*.

As I was trying to describe how it felt, she said, "Yes, it's all very liminal."

I distinctly remember my curiosity was piqued as I grabbed my journal and a pen.

"What was that word again? Can you spell it?"

(I, too, had never heard the word liminal before!)

The literal meaning of limin is *threshold*. It was most commonly used in ancient Greek culture to refer to a person being inducted into an order. At the ceremony, they were no longer an initiate, but they were also not yet a member. They were this whole other thing as they stood on the threshold. Before they stepped from backstage onto the stage, they prepared themselves for this change.

As I grew to recognize liminal spaces all around me and throughout our lives and stories, I realized this threshold moment just scratched the surface of the liminal experience. Liminality describes not just the moment in time when you make the step in a new direction but rather the entirety of the time it takes you to traverse the transition. The truth of life is that many transitions take time. So, while there is movement associated with this threshold space, it happens on a spectrum of both instantaneous to infinite.

I wonder if you would begin to get curious with me. Stop and think about this concept of liminality and where you might see it around you, woven into your life.

All throughout history, society has been brought into order through ritual and routine. It is what brings culture to a people. Our ways of life are marked by our cycles, seasons, and celebrations. Transitions and change, liminality, are both what form our stories and move them forward.

The seasons of spring and autumn, when nature is so actively on full display of waxing or waning, are beautiful examples of liminality. Trees no longer look like bare bones reaching to an empty sky as they do in winter, nor are they full and lush as in the height of summer. In their liminal stages, they are either speckled with bright buds or languishing with autumnal color dripping to the ground. If ever in need of a sign of liminality, look to the trees. When the harvest is brought in for our feasting, and the pies cool on the window sill or the solstice sun returns to warm the earth, we enjoy great times of pausing to celebrate and take notice. People honor and create traditions around these times to mark the difference we feel. We light fires, we dance, we cook and eat lavish meals, make love and promises.

The physical spaces *within* nature also show us the betweenness of things. The shoreline is a perfect example - always in its flux of tides - water in a constant state of motion as it creeps up to hug the sea wall or bares to us the pungent-smelling universe of life along the shoreline. The edge of the woods or mouth of a cave where we cannot see what lies beyond is so very liminal that even the imagery of a yawning dark mouth of a cave or a path can give us the shivers. The phases of the moon ever consistent in their change. The time of day I mentioned earlier.

The gloaming, that twilight, dusky time when the world is not fully awake, yet not sleeping. This has long been held to be a mystical time when the veil between the physical and spiritual is thinned. These are magical times and places where you get a sense of special energy and possibility.

Let's explore some of these places together as they present in our lives. Places we might not fully understand right now within ourselves. There is an internal mystery inside us all, as well. One we will learn to see and cultivate with care.

Celtic spirituality, in its beginning and still now, honors these cycles and seasons as special events in the year. Making meaning out of them and opening ourselves up to listening and marking these special times. Paying attention to the changes in the world and the changes within ancient monastic traditions, like feast days and the Wheel of the Year, likewise regard these liminal times. The Desert Mothers and Fathers in ancient Rome purposefully took themselves out of society to create liminality for themselves, residing in caves away from town to experience what they would. A sacred space where special things could happen. What did they know that we have forgotten?

Nature and spirituality are not the only arenas with a wide display of liminal spaces. There are physical places we create in our lives that are in between places. Many of them have the reputation of being uncomfortable. Think of places like a doctor's office, waiting rooms, or elevators! Do you immediately get that prickly sense on the back of your shoulders from the discomfort you feel in those places? Nobody talking, no one making eye contact, and everyone waiting. Liminal spaces are the waiting places. Other examples of liminality in physical spaces are bridges, tunnels, airports, parking lots, and hallways. (Spooky movie scene, anyone?!) Doorways, of course, with their lentils and welcome mats, are classic thresholds.

Are you starting to see how liminality is everywhere?

However, liminality is not just physical; it is also metaphorical and also represents times in your life and in your story. You can even experience times of life that feel liminal. Ages and stages. Seasons of being. This is where liminality gets *really* interesting!

We celebrate all manner of stages in childhood, especially coming of age. Every culture and religion throughout time has something special to celebrate and mark the coming of age. Quinceañeras and Bat/Bar Mitzvahs, Sweet Sixteens, and Catechism. What are the coming-of-age rites and rituals from your lived experience?

We mark the beginnings of adulthood – being "launched" - as crossing a threshold. We create a liminal season of engagement before marriage. The tradition of the groom carrying his wife across the threshold of their new home marks the beginning of their new life together. Before we are parents, we travel through the very liminal season of pregnancy. You are not yet a parent, but no longer without child. The nursery sits empty, yet that child's life fills your thoughts and days. We have names for stages of life like Midlife Crisis and Empty Nest. All tremendously liminal in essence.

Tribal cultures commonly create a rite of passage for boys to become men. The rituals read like a ramped-up version of fraternity hazing. Life or death is often on the line as they - sometimes in isolation or sometimes with a group of other initiates - live apart from their village and families. Usually, they are sent to live on the edge of town, alone, in a makeshift hut created just for this temporary time. Typically, hunting is involved, or some sort of proof of valor and strength, and the initiate is welcomed back into society as a man. He is looked at differently, treated differently, and given different perks and permissions because of his new status. He had not only crossed the threshold but endured the transition and returned *transformed*. This is the promise of each great journey.

Girls experience a much more private, internal initiation into womanhood with the dramatic changes that come with their first menstruation. The female body marks the changes and enters into a liminal cycle that will last for decades to come.

It is the Hero's Journey, in essence, which always begins with a call to change, followed by resistance to change, and an inevitable movement forward toward a new horizon. How the Hero handles their journey has a lot to do with the mindset they have when they set out. Often, the Hero is rigid and only sees one possible outcome or one type of success. Usually, our heroes are convinced that the good outcomes are not their lot, so there isn't a lot of hope in their hearts as they set out.

When Bilbo is first visited by a certain "meddling wizard" and a company of unruly dwarves, he scoffs at the idea of leaving his comfortable hole in the ground and rejects the idea that anything good could come from this type of change. Bilbo's reluctance to be the hero of his own story mirrors our own reticence to see transition and change as an opportunity.

When you walk through the transitions of life convinced of only one proper outcome, you limit yourself to only one way being the "right" way. This rigidity causes the lion's share of the struggle. If you consign yourself to only two paths, you create enormous pressure for yourself to get it right, fearing what will happen when and if you don't.

As we follow any hero through the classic cycle, we see that they are joined by comrades and mentors; they struggle through many challenges and choices - fighting the mythical dragons along the way. There will always be dragons. But there will also always be magic moments.

Every hero returns changed. Every hero makes it through the transition - returning with great rewards for daring to take the adventure. But not every hero weathers the journey as well as others.

In the classic children's movie, *The NeverEnding Story*, we see Atreyu start out as the ultimate willing hero. He travels to the Ivory Tower of his own accord, willing to use all his power and prowess to fight The Nothing so the Empress and all of Fantasia can be saved. But even he loses heart along the way. Because he held tight to one idea being the only way to save the land. He hits a wall when that one idea cannot seem to come to fruition. Atreyu eventually benefits from the wise help of a mentor, the Southern Oracle, who shows him that the way forward is one he could not have imagined. It is through seeing his true self reflected back to him in the form of a human boy who isn't even from Fantasia. Atreyu's binary thinking trapped him in a place without curiosity and, therefore, without choice.

I will show you how to see the adventures of liminality as an opportunity for living your best and most authentic self by looking at how Both/And thinking leads you to choice and voice - ultimately giving you compassion and connection for yourself and others. I have walked this journey, and am so happy to act as your guide, showing you what I have learned through lived experience.

You will not only walk through life avoiding a lot of the overwhelm, you will know how to deal with it when it does hit. You will also seek out new situations with curious anticipation rather than dread, knowing the liminal spaces will lead you to stretch and grow! You will get so much more out of life because your capacity for discomfort will be increased, and you will live fully in the moment as it unfolds, making choices and moving forward with much more grace, calm, and strength. New horizons are yours!

Will you accept the quest?

THE 4-LETTER F-WORD

"I was at a crossroads that I did not ask for. I didn't want to be there. I wanted things to stay the same."
~ Christine Paintner

I started paying attention to the liminal spaces and places in life around the same time I started my healing journey at the start of 2021. No small coincidence, I think.

We were all in the throes of the Covid Pandemic, and I am sure that is part of what precipitated my engagement with a therapist. Like many of you, with many touchstones of normalcy removed, I found myself at the end of my tether. There is a reason TeleHealth boomed during that disjointed period of time.

I felt very alone and overwhelmed. I was confused as to why I was behaving the way I was behaving and why my reactions to things seemed to be so intense. I felt trapped like there was nothing different to be done. I had very little margin for discomfort. Nor did I have much hope because I could not *imagine* things looking any other way. I felt tremendously unstable, and I despaired.

Maybe this is where you are now, or you know a time when you have been in that place. Life is like a roller coaster with the same familiar stops whizzing by on repeat. If we have been there before, we experience a form of tension and dread that we will be back there again. We want to avoid that pain.

In early '21, I found myself hiding in my kitchen pantry, mindlessly stuffing food into my mouth until I hurt. Not hungry. Even a little bewildered. Sort of numb and completely on auto-pilot... almost like an out-of-body experience. Eating, eating, eating. Physically bursting and hurting but not quite feeling full. But definitely feeling unhinged. *What is going on?*

What was going on, I soon learned, was that I was outside my window of tolerance. I had no capacity to be uncomfortable. I had been over-functioning for a very long time in an effort to deal with the discomfort I felt from all the transitions and challenges that life had dealt me. And that, my friends, is simply not a sustainable way to live.

I just couldn't go on like that.

I could not continue to live with rigid, binary thinking that gave me no imagination for how else things might look. Where there is no imagination for a different way, there is no hope. I had no choice, and so I had no voice. I could not be curious about myself or others because I was so insatiably focused on getting the one-way right, which is a never-ending loop of perceived failure because it is a fallacy - *there is no right way.*

I found myself in uncomfortable places with no ability to help myself seek comfort or strength.

Looking back on this time, the thing that captures my attention the most is how I really thought everything was *fine.* I was making it all work, keeping all the plates spinning.

Working full-time (more than full-time as all teachers do, especially if you look at the work we take home and all the "volunteering"), managing the kids, and running the house mostly on my own while my husband traveled extensively for work... and putting on a shiny, happy face for all of it! I was *fine.*

I don't recall a lot of self-reflection or introspection at this time. I really didn't see all the moving parts. Or at least, if I saw them, I didn't see the *significance* of them - and I certainly didn't see my *responses* to them. I was too busy surviving.

I remember reading an article that was published by a life insurance company. It outlined the top 10 most stressful situations or times in life, and I was in the middle of several of them. But I thought everything was *fine*. I was *fine*. My marriage was *fine*. My kids were *fine*.

Are you *"fine,"* too?

"I am fine" is a mindset. In reality, your house is burning down around you as you cook another low-carb, gluten-free, lean-protein perfect dinner for your family. "I am fine" is a disconnected mindset. We are not fine. *"Fine,"* is our new 4-letter F-word, friend.

In hindsight, of course, I can see I wasn't *fine*. None of it was. I was not really the best teacher I could have been. I did not have the capacity most days to be very present with my students, and if I did, that certainly took whatever energy I had for the day away from my own children. This might be the era where my three kiddos cooked up the term "mean mommy." *Bless their hearts.*

But I earned it. I would regularly snap at them and berate them. Each morning and evening, a litany of nagging for them to do *all the things*: "Clean your rooms," "Do your homework," "Hurry up!" "Put your shoes on!" ... "Are you crazy?! Take a jacket with you today!" Not often did I have the ability or awareness to slow down for them and be present.

How full is your family's schedule? Is running to soccer and dance and endless extracurricular activities doing more to harm than to enhance your children's lives and the tone of your family's lived experience? There is pressure today to have our children (over) scheduled and involved in a variety of after-school activities. Often, it involves eating in the car, staying up late to finish homework, and constant *weeping and gnashing of teeth* to get it all done. Might we stop and consider if this is serving us well?

My marriage, too, was systematically *fine*. But *fine* is not healthy. There was no true engagement or connection happening on a level deeper than budget talks or daily chats. No sense of partnership or belonging. And we even went on dates and overnight trips on our own! It's not like we were actively ignoring each other! But we were each so disconnected from the fact that we were living in a triggered state and not at all our authentic selves; we simply didn't have that to give to each other.

I never talked to anyone about any of this, though, because *it never occurred to me that there was anything to talk about.*

This is just life, right?

Then why does something just not feel right? Why am I not at peace? Why this internal dissonance telling me something is not okay?

The tips & tricks that were offered to help me *do* better and *be* better and *get it right* just fell apart after a while. I've tried them all.

- *Maybe I need to get up even earlier! ...Or stay up later?*
- *I could get more organized! 15 minutes at a time.*
- *I could prep my meals better. Meal prepping! That will help, for sure!*
- *I could de-clutter the house! Does this item bring me joy??*
- *I could plan my lessons better. I see a new day planner in my future.*
- *I could make a few more colorful charts about all the things that kids needed to do.*
- *I just need to pray more and have more faith. I could wake up earlier for more bible reading and prayer time. Prayer will fix this.*
- *We are all fine!*

Sound familiar? If you just *do more*... If you could just *be more!* Keep striving. Don't give up! *Rest is for the wicked.* You will get it *right*, and everything will be... *fine*. And you will live your #bestlife.

If you really dig in here and look at the thinking behind "making everything better," it points to the logic that you think everything is *not* actually okay. If you are working hard to *be* fine, then everything is *not* fine.

Society *normalizes* this impossible way of being, which doesn't allow us to see it in its proper place as a problem that needs to be addressed. Even the best of us will eventually crumble under the untenable pressure of feeling like we have to get it all right all the time.

The truth is binary thinking is damaging. It is damaging for two reasons.

Binary thinking says there is one right way and the problem with that is if you don't happen to do everything right, you are always going to be beating yourself up about something. This leads to a lack of self-compassion. Not living from a place of self-compassion is not living in your most true, authentic self. Essentially, you are at war with that self.

The other result of being trapped in binary thinking is the constant place of fear you must operate from. Fear leads to a lack of self-trust. You convince your-self you only have one way to get things right; you live in fear you will fail - *as we all do* - and when you fail to do the one thing you thought was right, you are only left with the feeling you've done something wrong. You are less likely to think you'll get it "right" in the future. Most of the time, this is the point where people double down and try harder. See the list above.

This vicious cycle steals from you any hope of authentic living. Authenticity requires both a love of self and trust of self. Self-compassion gets curious about what brings life and explores choices. Self-compassion has a voice and boundaries. Self-trust doesn't allow you to throw yourself under the bus when there is a decision to be made. It understands that multiple outcomes can all lead to life and wellness.

Liminal space is overwhelming when you have a binary mindset because there is only one "right way," which leads to fear of getting it wrong.

There is a better way. Let me show you now...

Partial Solutions - Part of the Problem

Before we go there, I want to address two partial solutions that often occur to people in transition because I think it might seem natural to call on these ideas for help, however limited they are.

You could make your life smaller. Sometimes, that is the solution. Less to deal with makes it easier to deal with each thing. There is value in taking things off the table. Honestly, this is where I started. I canceled commitments and stepped away from social circles.

And it did help! I could manage my fewer spinning plates better. Less wobbles all around.

There are two major limitations to this solution, though. First, most of us just simply aren't able to make this happen because of logistics. Life doesn't stop. - We can't quit our jobs, stop parenting our kids, stop nursing the sick, throw our arms up and make the cosmos stop turning, or... fill in the blank. Many of these transition times are thrust upon us. - We did not choose them...so.

The other downside to this solution is that making your life smaller *shrinks* it. It usually also comes with the side effect of fewer people and connections. When you are already struggling, it can be risky to remove relationships. If the relationships are toxic or lack boundaries, it could be a beneficial partial solution. But if it leads you into further isolation, it could be harmful. It makes the road ahead much more challenging. We will talk more about this later in Chapter 8 and consider how we need a connection to thrive on this journey.

Another partial solution is to look at the transitions in our lives as seasons and focus on the light at the end of the tunnel. *This, too, shall pass.* Again, there is value here! The concept of seasons is very powerful and alluring. It is a great Truth that cannot be discounted. Things are only here for a time. We can take strength and hope in the fact that things will not always be like this!

The limitation of this way of thinking as the *only* solution, however, is that it does nothing for my ability to cope better in the *midst* of the transition. Liminal spaces are constantly presenting themselves - shifting in and out of our reality regularly. There are many of them at any given time, and that is just modern life. We won't get away from that.

Takeaways:

Liminal space is overwhelming when you have a binary mindset because there is only one "right way," which leads to fear of getting it wrong.

2

A BETTER WAY

"Authenticity (is) the quality of being true to oneself and the capacity to shape one's own life from a deep knowledge of that self."
- Gabor Mate

The drive up to Whidbey Island from the Kitsap Peninsula, where I live, includes crossing a floating bridge, driving up the edge of the Olympic Peninsula, taking a short ferry ride across to the island itself, and another drive down the island. Welcome to Puget Sound Living. 170 islands, 10 ferry routes, and thousands of bridges.

I signed up for a Rewilding Retreat!

I had crossed a pivotal threshold in my liminal journey and was actively seeking to put myself in places of growth, getting curious and having an internal dialogue over what I wanted my life to look like.

What I had set out to do for myself this day was place myself in proximity to that which is unfamiliar. I wanted to do something that resonated *with* me, *for* me - and outside of my comfort zone. I was not quite the expert in curiosity that I am now. The great thing is curiosity is something to be seized - no skill set is required. So, I was seizing an opportunity.

I was headed to The Storyhouse at the Whidbey Institute. And I was late. I pulled my car into the far back edges of the packed dirt parking lot. I quickly used the outdoor facilities. I say *quickly,* mostly because I have an utter phobia of portable toilets. I cast my eyes upward, trying not to see anything but the essentials. This was a day for *brave hovering!* Look at me, rewilding already! (or, could read, "Wild, indeed.")

As I scurried up to the cabin on the edge of the glade, I heard drumming. And chanting! Oh, boy. I have never. My old internal narrative was telling me that drums are for tribal cultures and chanting is for monasteries. Where am I? What have I gotten myself into?

I have certainly crossed a threshold into a new and unfamiliar place.

But what a place of warmth and welcome I found as I entered. Thirteen smiles all around. The leader, Mary DeJong, founder of Waymarkers who was running the retreat, shined on me with such a beatific smile it put me immediately at ease. As did her warm hands that wrapped around mine as she said, "You're here now. Just breathe." Oh, wow. This woman has my number.

Happy sigh.

So breathe, I did. I breathed as I sat in a circle with other women who had also bravely stepped into the woods on this day to get in touch with our authentic selves and hear what Mary had to say about "crossing over from Western world boundaries into a recovery of ancient ways of being in relationship with the Sacred through creation." *This* is what we had signed up for.

Before applying the knowledge and practices in this book, I never would have had the ability to take this adventure for myself, nor by myself. It honestly wouldn't even have occurred to me to do something just because I wanted to do it. Life was so focused on what I could do for other people and getting it all right, and not a lot of care (or even curiosity) for what shimmered for me.

When was the last time you did something for yourself, by yourself? It is not something we often give ourselves permission to do when we are busy striving to do *all the things.*

Without the knowledge I share with you in the following chapters, I lived in such a reactive state that I did not have the capacity or extra margin to take on a lot of newness without great cost to myself. The awareness I now have of my own responses and reactions and freedom from rigid thinking is invaluable in experiencing life to its fullest. Authentic life.

That's what I want to show you so you can thrive in purposeful living from a place of authenticity. If we look at authenticity, as I said above, as a deep knowing of oneself and working from that place of knowledge and intimacy to make choices and decisions that most align with your core self, we see that authenticity requires both a love of self and trust of self and leads you to explore all the choices of how things *could* be.

What hope that brings! What freedom! You see you have a vast amount of riches laid at your feet to choose from. You use your voice to call upon that which appeals to the highest good in your heart, and you create a way of life around it. You draw up healthy boundaries to lovingly protect that way of life, and you exercise your agency over all of it.

This doesn't mean things are perfect. Nor will you delude yourself into thinking all your choices were ideal. You know life is messier than that, and when the less-than-ideal outcome disappoints you or others, you are able to hold in open hands that such is the way of life, and you will not be destroyed by it. Even if you do deem it a mistake, you acknowledge that you can make mistakes - you are allowed to. Because you are enough - you chose self-compassion.

From the moment you picked up this book, you entered another liminal space. You have crossed a threshold that has the potential of putting you into some dis-ease and whisking you away on adventure. I will act as both your mentor and your boon companion along the way, as every hero needs.

And you, of course, are the hero of this story - your own story.

We have some stops to make along this journey, and we will look at them in three parts: Preparing Your Path, Charting Your Path, and Navigating Your Path.

As we **Prepare Your Path**, I want to show you some key things about the way your brain works to keep you safe! When you put that together with the understanding that binary thinking instigates fear, you have a powerful insight into your responses to liminal spaces. So, I will show you the key to flexibility with Both/And thinking.

We will then take time to do some really personal exploration in **Charting Your Path**. Only you know the specific places you are in transition in your life right now, and how long you've been in those places. You will have a chance to practice the pause and peer into your life, considering all the moving parts and your responses to them - and whether or not you might be holding on to some rigid thinking around those places.

Finally, in **Navigating Your Path**, we get to look ahead together at what liminal life is like when you become curious with yourself and others. Now that you are no longer adhering to binary thinking, you have a choice. What will you decide brings you life, and what drains you of life? What connections will you seek out, and where will you find belonging? These are the treasures waiting for you further down the path.

At the end of Navigating Your Path, I've included a very practical chapter on Mapping Your Choices. The invitation here is to explore the specific things that are challenging you right now! The mapping will give you a chance to reflect on the stress responses you uncovered in the Preparing Your Path section, as well as practice the Both/And language you learn in Chapter 4 for self-care and connection.

I promise to show you how to navigate the liminal spaces in life so you can embrace the Both/And mindset and gain choice through curiosity, which will result in living your most authentic life.

Takeaways:

Liminal space becomes an opportunity when you have a Both/And mindset. This way of thinking allows for multiple outcomes. When there are multiple outcomes, we have a choice. When we have a choice, we can become curious (with ourselves and others) about what serves us best, so we gain voice and agency, leading to authentic living.

PREPARING
YOUR PATH

3
KNOW THYSELF

"We're not ourselves when we're triggered - we become who we think we need to be to survive. And when we're constantly being triggered, our identity can start to slip away - - because our personality and values are constantly getting hijacked by fight-or-flight reflexes."
- Dr. Glenn Patrick Doyle

In my early 40s, I was determined to become a hobby farmer and homesteader. I had a 1,000-square-foot garden, wore denim overalls, kept chickens and ducks, had my eyes on some goats, read articles on how to make my own bread and soap (I got the bread part down), and did the math on how many greens beans I would need to "put away" to last my (then) family-of-four through the winter. To make this math a reality, I needed to learn the subtle art of *canning*.

I found a large pressure cooker for sale on a second-hand website and went to pick it up. The elderly couple selling this large silver monster did not have a handy instruction booklet, but they pointed here and there at the various knobs and gadgets and assured me it would all be okay.

I saw the two of them in my mind's eye as we were driving away... Miracle Max and his wife:

"Think it'll work?" asks the crone.

Billy Crystal's character says, "Not a chance!" as they keep smiling and waving.

"Have fun storming the castle, kids!"

Pressure cookers can be dangerous if you don't manage them properly. You need to moderate the pressure that is building and release it at certain times and in certain ways. I will be honest - it was very intense for me! I literally pulled a dining room chair over and sat in the middle of the kitchen, staring at this thing without blinking for the hours it took to process the green beans! It was new to me - eons away from being second nature - and I thought if I gave it my *full* attention, I was more likely to avoid a disaster.

The only other time I'd stared that long or that hard at anything was my firstborn child in the hospital the hours after birth. For much the same reasons, I suppose!

Disaster averted. No green bean wallpaper. (Also, a healthy, well-adjusted young man. Both wins!)

Learning proper use of the pressure cooker to avoid disaster is how I came to feel about brain science. It is important to know how the brain works. In fact, let's not even neutralize the idea by calling it "the brain." As if we are talking about some generalized brain out there! *My brain.* I believe it is important to know how *my brain* works. After all, it is the one I have to live with! And just like with the pressure cooker, I'd like to feel a bit more proficient in using it!

The most important thing I learned about the brain in all the reading and research I did, and classes I took, was how it responds when it doesn't feel safe - and the fact that it *always* wants to feel safe!

As you know from Chapter 2, when we try to traverse the liminal spaces in our lives while holding on to binary thinking, we throw ourselves into a vicious cycle of fear and failure.

Each transition or change in life leads us on this cycle. Every "yes," every "no." Each and every "not yet" and "not now" - - as well as all the unexpected events thrust and lobbed at us by life. Each one is its own journey with discomfort and liminal nuance. It feels unsafe when you only have one shot at *getting it right.*

When we do not perceive warmth, welcome, or safety, there are very deep triggers within us that create physiological responses. Responses we may not be aware of or even feel like we can control. Remember when I talked about hiding in closets, stuffing myself, or doing all the things to be *fine*?! If you relate to that, then hold on to your hat - this next part might blow you away.

Sometimes, these natural responses cause us to try to run from our problems or avoid them - mentally or physically. Often, these responses can create a feeling of angst within us that makes us throw up our dukes. At times, we can't even find the words to say. We stare off into the distance, check out, and get exhausted or depressed. And sometimes we respond by trying to please everyone around us to make sure our environment is safe because everyone is happy.

Let's look at some details around these responses while remembering that they're goal is to keep us safe - they are not *bad*, so let's not moralize them that way. They are simply not always necessary or helpful, and we need to be able to recognize when they are occurring so we have Choice around our behaviors and responses.

FIGHT:

The fight response in its literal sense can obviously be - fists flying, angry words, yelling, and accusations - it can also look like other aggressive behaviors such as refusing to hear someone else's point of view, needing to dominate and control other people, demanding perfection from yourself or those around you, pursuing power and control, bullying, criticizing, dictating. Its goal is self-preservation at all costs.

Explosive tempers and outbursts are overt, but some of these behaviors are subversive if carried out by people with quieter personalities. The Fight response in them can go unnoticed until you look at specific tendencies like the effort they put into controlling their surroundings and the people in their lives. They are still aggressive; they are just passive-aggressive. Are you a fighter?

FLIGHT:

Again, there are overt ways this response can display itself, as well as less obvious ways. You need to get out of the house, leave the meeting, walk away from the conversation. When you say the wrong thing and feel like fleeing a situation at all costs, that is the flight response in you.

We also run away in our heads. We become workaholics, always on the go. Staying for extra shifts and overtime, working out while we are not working, and volunteering when we aren't doing either of those.

Or we worry a lot and become over-analytical. We run from being present by ruminating, overthinking, over-analyzing. We call it playing chess in our house. It's thinking several moves ahead and all possible outcomes.

We cannot just sit with ourselves, or others really. We just can't sit still. The hyper-active rushing around and doing all the things feels very obsessive and compulsive in nature. These are the people who are hard to have a conversation with because they just can't stay in the moment. Is this you?

FREEZE:

Also referred to as "faint or flop", the mental image that always comes to mind for me when I think of this stress response is a deer in headlights. However, again, that is just what it would look like in its most simple, obvious form. When you look at what freeze or faint looks like in the mind, it can look like depression.

Are you checked out or detached? I always know when this stress response is hitting me because I feel an irrational sleepiness and a need for quiet and closed-eyes. I reach decision-fatigue, can't process things that are being said to me, and it literally feels like I'm shutting down. I feel an imminent collapse on the way.

If you often avoid human contact, withdraw and isolate from people, struggle to make decisions, or even to get out of bed for the day - this might be your stress response. Putting clothes on, deciding what to eat, showering even…it all feels like too much. Sound familiar?

FAWN:

I'm going to talk about this stress response in more detail because it is absolutely the biggest dragon women do battle with today.

The best way to recognize those responding to their stress from this place of fawning is the constantly tired smile they have plastered on their face when they are around other people. These are the "shiny happy people" who fly completely under the radar as having stress responses at all. We often do not see that the people-pleasers are responding to a need for felt safety. But, oh, they are. Inwardly, they're thinking, *If I can say "yes" to everything anyone asks me to do and keep my opinions to myself, I will be okay.* And they are probably not even aware of it. (Again, this is just life, right?)

These are people who will be uncomfortable if you ask them their own opinion, or even really try to focus the conversation on them at all. Whatever anyone else wants, thinks, or says is A-OK with them! They are very concerned with what everyone thinks of them and will have zero boundaries to honor themselves. They have a hard time naming their feelings and often feel a loss of identity and lack of belonging. They feel ultimately responsible for other people's feelings and reactions.

They are "cooperative and appeasing, unassertive, patient, unexpressive of negative emotions (particularly anger), and compliant with external authorities... excessively nice, pleasant to a fault, uncomplaining and unassertive." Gabor Maté, The Myth of Normal.

They are always there first with a casserole in hand, always stay until closing, always volunteering, always leading. There is an irrational need to control and an enormous effort is put into micromanaging all the details of the situation - their kids, their spouse, other people. Masquerading as self-effacing servitude, they call all the shots and will endlessly strive for this comfortable position.

Today, it is the common way of women to hyper-function in response to societal pressures. We need to do *all the things* and be Pinterest-Perfect. They run the auctions. They chair your committees. They organize those bake sales. They are the Room Moms.

The Den Mothers. The CEOs. The Boss Babes. The Party Planners. The Over Achievers. The Perfectionists. And from the outside, they look like they have their shit together!

This is absolutely my M.O. for stress response. But I will be honest with you. As I did all of those amazing things, I didn't have my shit together. Very much not. Shit everywhere.

And here's the mic-drop: Society sees our excessive "helpfulness" as a virtue, making it a socially acceptable stress response. It is often encouraged and groomed in our young people and women in particular. The traits of an over-pleaser are often praised and thought of as strengths. Being the "good girl" is a harmful and damaging trauma response that many of us live with and perpetuate by making it into an actual *goal*.

What this actually gets you is a feast of loneliness, overwhelm, and fear with a side-dish of exhaustion. Aren't you just tired of the never-ending, all-encompassing doing of all the things for all the people just in an effort to "get it right?"

This way of being clearly does not serve us.

I could not continue to live in a way that perfected everyone else's experience of me and pleased others but left me completely out of the picture. There was no self-compassion, no self-trust. *No self*. Another thing missing was curiosity, therefore I had no choice nor voice.

We need to stop giving our brain a reason to feel unsafe.

Let's talk about the magic of Both/And thinking.

Takeaways:

We respond to the stress that comes with binary thinking the way we would any other stress in life. These are our default responses. We can have any of these responses at any given time, but you probably already know which common responses your brain usually goes to, don't you?

4

I CONTAIN MULTITUDES

"There is no try. There is only do or do not."
- Yoda

Before I have my much beloved and well-earned Nerd Card revoked, let me just say - *I love Yoda!* He rocks. Or - *"Love Yoda, I do."* So, let's take a step back and look at how and why he used this nugget of apparent wisdom in the Star Wars saga...

Yoda, the wise old mentor, is training our hero, Luke, a new Jedi Knight with a lot of power and little self-control, to go up against a great evil. He is trying to get Luke to *focus* and, ...get this, to *do everything right.* The future of the Galaxy depends upon it!

So, *okay*, if you ever find yourself defending the galaxy against the evil of your lost father you thought was dead your whole life but turns out was remade into a partial robot by the Evil Emperor and the fate of all that is good rests on your shoulders - get your shit together. Be as binary as possible so you get it all right and win the gold medal from the princess (who is really your sister, by the way - spoiler alert) in the end. Get down with your bad self! Luke's fight response was appropriate and even helpful in this situation.

You get the joke, but really - anyone who knows this beloved story well knows how very much Luke suffered from his inability to settle into his own skin and release rigid thinking. If you, like me, consider yourself to be just a normal person living an average life - not saving the galaxy - rigid thinking is harmful. Binary thinking, by definition, is a "black or white," "either/ or " mindset that leaves no in-between. It is fixed and rigid. *Only one way is right.* This simply does not serve us.

Let's look at how this mindset leads to fear and the need to control, and how duality uses extreme language before we move on to considering the freedom found in flexibility and the open-handed language used there, and how that can lead to self trust.

Fear and the need for control

Your brain is always seeking safety - as you learned in the last chapter. Of course, liminal places and spaces can often disrupt your perception of this basic need. When rigid, binary thinking is all you know, times of liminality and discomfort can really throw you into a tailspin. The very nature of liminality as we observed earlier in the book is that there is very little known and a lot of the unknown.

Safety is often found in what is familiar (even if the familiar is totally damaging) or what we feel is within our control. Binary thinking gives you a false sense of control by allowing you to focus on that "one way" you want to achieve to "get it right." It also simultaneously delivers a powerful sense of fear.

When you step into the trap of either-or thinking, you're immediately doomed. If there's "one way" to get it right, and you don't... well, where does that leave you? Getting it wrong. Failing. Loss.

<u>Extreme Language</u>

Binary thinking uses very extreme language. Some examples of this type of thinking:

> "I failed my driver's test. I'm _never_ going to drive again."
> "I _always_ get tongue-tied when I try to talk to him."
> "I _can't ever_ speak to them again."
> "_All_ my friends laughed at me. _No one_ gets me. I am _totally_ alone."
> "She voted for who?! Well, _clearly,_ we can't be friends anymore."
> "I don't think I'm _allowed_ to do that..."

"You're not loading the dishwasher _correctly_.
Ugh, I'll just _do it myself_."

Do you notice the extremes? Binary thinking pushes us to either end of the spectrum: _always, never, all, everyone, no one._ If you have raised a teenager or remember what it was like to be one, you will recognize the immaturity and fixed thinking of binary language. It is common in kids because they don't have the emotional maturity yet to know what to do with the gray areas in life.

What this type of language does for your ability to deal with ambiguity cannot be overstated. Our brain believes what we tell it. When we use such extreme language, we are not allowing for imagination, curiosity or choice. We are telling ourselves it is only _this_ way, it can only _be_ this way, it _will_ only be this way. We create a stuck, fixed way of being and thinking when we process with extreme, dualistic language.

Rigid thinking does not account for the complexity of life... or people. We are all complex. I love this quote by Walt Whitman, taken from _Song of Myself_: "Do I contradict myself? Very well, then, I contradict myself. I am large. I contain multitudes." "I contain multitudes." Absolutely.

Another thing rigid thinking doesn't account for is the fact that multiple outcomes of any given situation can be acceptable. And, moreso, often actually preferable.

Both/And mindset

The greatest boost on my road to healing has been sweeping aside the rocks of rigidity and treading a smoother path of flexibility. This means I refuse to be motivated by the fear of what-ifs and the fear of people's opinions any longer. This means embracing the "Both/And" mindset - accepting what is and trusting that what-will-be is not bigger than me. Both/And acknowledges that there are many ways each turn of the path can lead somewhere good because I trust myself to navigate any given situation. Even and especially the imperfect ones. I can trust the future because I can trust myself.

I discovered my favorite analogy for Both/And thinking in Patrick Rothfuss' best selling fantasy fiction book, *The Name of the Wind*.* The hero, Kvothe, learns the power of his *alar* from his mentor, Ben, while riding along in a wagon.

The wise old Ben places a rock in young Kvothe's hand and asks him to simultaneously believe with firmness that the rock will both drop and stay in mid-air when he opens his hand.

Our hero sweats and strains for hours as he trains his mind to fully accept that both realities can exist at the same time. Wow! Integration, anyone?

Both/And is like this. It can acknowledge and accept that my situation can be okay and not okay at the same time. The overriding power is knowing *I'm* OK, no matter what happens around me. I have freedom and flexibility in the new openness that Both/And brings.

I love the illustration in The Name of the Wind because it acknowledges that establishing this fortitude, this strength of mind, is hard! It's a challenge. And... you can achieve it. You can do hard things. And *when* you accomplish it, you can be *kick-ass* proud.

Holding things loosely like this, you can choose the beauty of ambivalence. You have the ability to embrace dichotomy and the freedom it brings.

You can open your hands and let go of the need to control every moment and be okay with *not knowing*. This looseness leads to a beautiful way of living. A much softer, more gentle, and loving way of being towards yourself and others. I can accept people for who they are, myself for who I am, life for what it is - and dance among the messiness of it all. I can even be okay with how they load the dishwasher.

<u>Both/And language</u>

Both/And thinking uses a whole different set of vocabulary than we saw in the realm of rigidity earlier. Take these phrases, for example:

"This is hard, but I can do hard things."

"I'm not good at this... yet."

"This is not going well today. Ok. I'll try again another day."

"What a mess. I really ruined that. I'm not perfect, though. And that's ok!"

"Well, that certainly wasn't great. But, I made progress."

"I suck at this! Yep! AND... I'm good at other things."

Our 12-Step brothers and sisters would be proud. Progress, not perfection. Progress says it is okay to not get it right all the time and we don't have to be perfect. We just need to keep working on it. We don't even necessarily have to keep moving forward, because sometimes progress looks like two steps forward, three steps back. Shampoo, rinse, repeat.

Progress is not always about doing our best, believe it or not! "Our best" is a relative concept, isn't it? Sometimes, my best from yesterday is not accessible to me the next day. Each day, our best looks different. And bringing my very best each day just isn't sustainable. I can bring what I have today. That's what I can give. And that, too, is okay. I can do the things today that are within my scope of ability or my realm of control. I can live day-by-day, moment-by-moment, making choices that concern myself and my wellbeing.

Multiplicity mindset

When we reject the rigid, open ourselves to the possibilities in Both/And thinking, and accept what is, we have created the perfect place of growth for a multiplicity mindset. We can see that there are many different ways each liminal path can take us. Although some might be easier or shorter or more convenient than others, all outcomes will be okay- because *you* are OK. You've got this.

If there are more than one acceptable path, it opens the door for curiosity. I can have a conversation with myself about what *might* be. I can see that many paths can lead to acceptable outcomes and that a certain degree of messiness and imperfection exists on every path, too! And that's okay! It can be Both/And.

When we see the world in a flexible, open-handed way, suddenly, there is a beautiful freedom that unfolds as we are allowed to rest in the luminous safety and unshakable security that is brought about by Both/And thinking, overriding any residual fear we held onto with rigidity.

How do you "hold onto" Both/And? It seems contra-dictory, right? Well, we do so with loose fingers and open palms. This is not the clenched, tight, death-grip of fear and control. This is the glorious birthing of something new - and you must breathe through it to make it work.

When we approach life with a flexible mindset, we are able to receive things that come towards us with more curiosity than condemnation. With more daring and less dread. We are not immediately jumping ship when we experience the dissonance of paradox and limbo. We hold the space well.

We are okay when we are not in control or we don't know what lies ahead because we trust ourselves enough to deal with whatever comes when it comes. Instead of obsessively thinking of what *might* happen, trust yourself to handle the situation (insert dreaded conversation, impending disaster, or random fear here) *if and when* it ever actually happens.

The benefit of flexible Both/And language and thought processes is that we know we are safe and well in many different outcomes. We aren't holding on to that fear of failure anymore, thinking that we must get it just one right way to be OK.

Your dualistic thinking has been released and replaced with the wonderfully soft and open hands of flexibility. You know that you can accept what is without the need to control it or fear it. What's more, now you can even lean into the unknown. You are well on your way to living as your authentic self.

. . .

Takeaways:

A fixed, rigid mindset leads to fear and the need to control, and this duality uses extreme language. There is freedom found in flexibility and the open-handed language used there, that can lead to self-trust.

CHARTING
YOUR PATH

5
YOU CAN'T UN-SEE IT

"Let's, here, take liminality as that which causes emotional dissonance or discomfort for us because of some shift or change in our situation."
- Victor Turner

On some journeys, we stop and smell the roses. On this journey, we are going to stop and inventory our liminal spaces!

I have found tremendous value in my own life when I sit down with a girlfriend or a therapist, and they ask, "So, what's new? How are you? What's going on in your life?" And they *truly* want to know.

I get to take a moment to pause and consider my answer. I'm always more likely to give a genuine response when I know the other person cares about the answer. And I'm often surprised!

I'm a verbal processor. When I unload and talk about *all the things*, the response is often: "Wow, that's a lot!"

I am seen and likewise can see myself. It really helps me stop and realize - *Wow, I really am dealing with a lot!*

Suddenly, things become clear!

It makes a lot more sense that I'm responding to life the way that I am.- I can see the places where I'm holding some rigidity of "getting it right." I can identify where my stress responses are kicking in. I notice where I'm not feeling safe and operating from a place of fear!

I'm constantly considering worst-case scenarios, snapping at the kids, grousing at my husband, not sleeping well at night, withdrawing from my friendships, eating things that don't fuel me well... ya, something is *off*! Hello, stress responses! I can suddenly see them all.

When we begin to evaluate all the many transitions we find ourselves in and the feelings that they elicit, we can start to see the magnitude of our struggle. The liminal places multiply with modern life, and therefore so do our responses. If we feel off-kilter and out of balance trying to traverse *one* transition, how much more so with many of them!? Enter, the overwhelm.

There is movement to liminality, but sometimes it is like molasses in wintertime – it is slow and creeping. So, we live in it. We live *through* it. We live in these places of insecurity and unknowing. We live with multiple layers of it all at once.

Sometimes, we choose these liminal times in life:

"I quit."
"I'm leaving."
"I got into college!"
"I'm traveling to Nigeria!"
"I'm pregnant!"
"I won!"

And sometimes these things happen to us:

"You're fired."
"The diagnosis came back."
"There's been an accident."
"It's broken."
"I'm sorry, she's gone."
"I lost."

You step over the threshold the moment you get the call or receive the text. Or someone sits you down and tells you, "Things are going to be different now."

<u>Record</u>

What stages and seasons of life are you currently walking through? Take a pause and consider all the aspects of your life right now that are new, temporary, or transitional. What changes have you recently experienced? What sudden changes have been thrust upon you? Just as the insurance article initially showed me all the major transitions I was walking through in my life, I want you to see the benefit of pausing to consider all your moving parts.

Work through this list (or grab the PDF version off my website at cajalonen.com) with a pencil in hand, and note the month/year you first experienced this shift beside each season or stage you identify being in right now. Noting the date will help you see what areas you have moved out of next time you take inventory, and what transitions are persisting.

You'll notice that some of these liminal spaces affect multiple areas of your life and are listed in more than one place.

JOB | CAREER

	Looking for a job
	Awaiting an employment interview result
	In negotiations
	Final stages of signing a contract
	New job, less than a year
	Taking on a new position of responsibility
	Recently fired, downsized or let go
	Currently at Boot Camp
	Currently deployed with the military
	Currently traveling for work
	Other:

RELATIONSHIPS | BELONGING

	Moving – New community
	Dating
	Engaged
	Newly wed
	Recently made a new friend
	Recently lost a friend
	Engaging a new social group
	New pet
	Loss of a pet
	Pregnant, partner pregnant
	Parenting an infant
	Parenting a toddler
	Parenting a teen
	Parenting a young adult
	Separated
	Going through a divorce
	Newly divorced
	New to therapy / new therapist
	Spouse or partner on deployment
	Family member with chronic illness
	Caregiver for family member
	Grieving the loss of a pregnancy
	Grieving a death, less than a year
	Grieving a death, less than five years
	Sitting suicide watch for a loved one
	Relationship in distress
	Other:

HEALTH

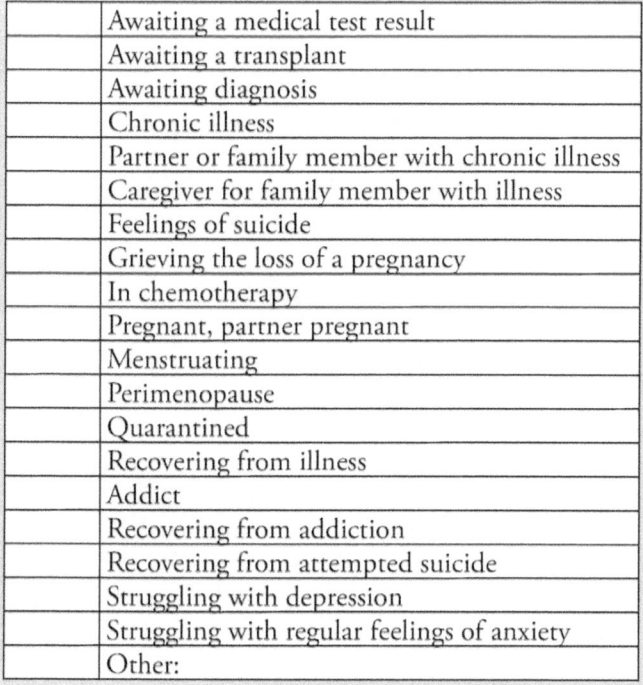

	Awaiting a medical test result
	Awaiting a transplant
	Awaiting diagnosis
	Chronic illness
	Partner or family member with chronic illness
	Caregiver for family member with illness
	Feelings of suicide
	Grieving the loss of a pregnancy
	In chemotherapy
	Pregnant, partner pregnant
	Menstruating
	Perimenopause
	Quarantined
	Recovering from illness
	Addict
	Recovering from addiction
	Recovering from attempted suicide
	Struggling with depression
	Struggling with regular feelings of anxiety
	Other:

SEASONS OF LIFE

	Coming of Age
	Preparing to go away to school
	Young adult
	Pregnant, partner pregnant
	Parenting an infant
	Parenting a toddler
	Potty training a child
	Parenting a teen
	Parenting a young adult
	Middle Age / Mid-life
	Empty Nest
	Caregiver for aging parents
	Retirement
	Other:
	Recovering from addiction
	Recovering from attempted suicide
	Struggling with depression
	Struggling with regular feelings of anxiety
	Other:

EDUCATION

	Awaiting an academic test result
	Awaiting acceptance to a school of choice
	Going back to school
	Going to a new school
	Learning something new – skill, craft or knowledge
	Other:

LOCATION

	Awaiting citizenship papers
	Expatriate
	Refugee
	Incarcerated
	Boot Camp
	Currently in a waiting room
	Currently on public transportation
	New home or community
	On vacation
	Other:

SPIRITUALITY

	Seeking faith
	Redefining your faith
	Engaging in new faith tradition
	New faith community
	Other:

ENVIRONMENTAL

	At the shore
	On a hike
	During the season of Spring or Fall
	Currently evening or twilight
	Other:

**Feel free to add your own situations - clearly there are so many that are unique to each of our lives, I could not even hope to list them all.

Pause for a moment.

Now, I'd like you to look back up at your list.

I know you have marked at least one because, after all, each season we live through is a liminal space.

If you marked 3 - 5 liminal spaces, I'm sure you can start to see where some of the overwhelm and stress responses are coming from.

Most people find themselves experiencing at least 5 and sometimes upwards to 10 in their lived experience at any given time. Whew! Just thinking about that.

That is *a lot*!

If that is you too, I see you. I get it. Life is just relentless, isn't it?

But if you're also walking through these times of transition completely unaware of the stress responses they trigger in you and approach each scenario with a binary mindset (telling yourself there's only *one* way you get each of those situations *right*), you add even more tension to the enormous amount of stress you are under.

But now that you know, now that you *see*, you can choose to do things differently.

As we discussed at the beginning of the book, sometimes the solution seems to be cutting back on things or just holding on for the light at the end of the tunnel. However, those partial solutions don't do anything to help us navigate the road better while we are on it.

Let's keep looking at your responses to these places and your mindset around each of them so that we can get you to a place of authenticity.

Consider Your Spaces

For each major liminal space you identify as part of your life right now, consider answering the following questions in some reflective journaling. Your insights and observations are key for ensuring lasting transformation because they allow you to process rather than merely acknowledge. Reflection is key to self-awareness. Self-awareness is key to lasting change.

Questions to consider about *each* liminal space you find yourself in:

Did you *choose* this, or do you see it as something that happened *to* you?

How long have you been in this space?

What are 3 emotion words you associate with this space?

When we perceive something happened *to* us that was not our choice, or we have been in a hard scenario for a long time, we tend to feel stuck or worse: trapped. Both of those feelings signal danger to your brain. No one likes to be trapped.

Consider re-framing your response with a mindset shift that puts you back in a position of power: "This is hard, but I can do hard things," or "I trust myself. I've got this."

Continue with this line of questioning:

Can you identify places of rigidity? What does that look like?

What have you told yourself is the "right" outcome of each scenario?

What are the other possible outcomes?

The "getting it right" line of thinking is especially tricky because we often don't realize we are doing it. Really slow down and get curious with yourself here. What success markers have you placed around each of the transitions you are walking through right now?

Here is where you get to stretch yourself a little.

How else could each situation turn out - and it still be okay? What you are trying to do here is create multiple little pathways in your brain that all feel safe?

If you can *imagine* multiple acceptable outcomes, you shed your binary thinking. You see that you have a choice, and the fear of failure diminishes. You increase your trust with yourself. *You've got this.*

This is the acceptance of an idea that we talked about in the Both/And chapter. A lot of peace comes when you release the ideas of impending disaster. When you stop obsessing over outcomes, you free yourself. You increase your margin for meeting the challenge for what it is in the moment. You give yourself (and others around you) the gift of being present. Truly authentic living is always present. Present with yourself as well as those around you.

Finally, ask yourself:

Do you see the ways in which your mind is responding to stress?

Do you behaviors which might be resulting from that stress response?

What language are you using with yourself? What can you replace it with?

This is the time to get really honest with yourself.

What were the stress responses from the earlier chapter that really resonated with you? Fight, Flight, Freeze or Fawn? How do you see yourself responding to all the moving parts in your life? Is it a mix? You are uniquely you and have specific ways only you will respond.

In the upcoming chapters I share some specific suggestions so you create healthy boundaries, find your Glorious, "Yes!," and increase connection with others. I'll also help you replace any *should* language with more honoring self-talk.

I'd like you to hold on to the insights you gained in this chapter. This section is all about Charting Your Path. The needs you identified here are the mindset shifts you will focus on in the upcoming Navigating Your Path section as you become curious with yourself and others.

Takeaway:

Liminal Life is a universal experience that once you see, you cannot un-see. It is happening all around us, all the time. Purposefully seeing this and acknowledging it is the powerful first step to responding to life with authenticity.

NAVIGATING YOUR PATH

6

SELF-CARE - A PRIMER

"May I never confuse shame with self-awareness. May my inspiration for change and transformation be rooted in love."
- Justin McRoberts

There is a charming little town in Montana called Whitefish. It is one of those tucked-away places dripping with so much Americana you want to stand up and place your heart over your hand and sing, "My Country 'Tis of Thee," like we all did back in elementary school every morning. Maybe it's just because my family was there on the 4th of July.

At the end of the incredible fireworks display set off in the middle of the lake where the sun had just set perfectly down the crevice between two dark blue hills in the distance, silence fell over the whole beach until it was broken by a man who stood and belted out the entire National Anthem while we all chimed in. I'm not kidding. It was like something out of a movie.

On the way back to the car, kids were riding their bikes while waving sparklers in the air. There was a general sense of bonhomie and unity oozing around all of us like some unseen spiritual force. It was lovely. It gave me chills.

Whitefish has a quaint little downtown area I suspect is just there for us tourists. It is a classic Main Street, featuring covered sidewalks held aloft by wooden poles, giving an Old West feel to the whole place. It is sprinkled with shops where you can buy Montana sweatshirts (I got mine in red) and eateries to plunk your family of four down for a rest and some home-style cooking.

One shop stood out to me and appealed to my irreverent sense of humor. It was full of beautiful journals and quality stationery, as well as lovely wine glasses and charming home decor... all with gorgeously lettered cuss words on them. *My people.*

One particular journal cover made me laugh out loud. I reached for it immediately. It was a cute little yellow, spiral-bound deal that featured these words in gold on the front: Get Your Shit Together.

Yes! I thought.

I was knee-deep in my healing journey at that point and was definitely getting my shit together. And it felt good. The admonition on the front of the journal felt like a cheer of encouragement to me at that time, and I treasured it. I filled that sucker up with words of hurt and healing for months.

One day, though, when I reached for it, I was in a particularly defiant state of mind. I had been working through some issues in therapy that showed me how the chronic trauma I experienced in my family of origin, coupled with my ultra-conservative faith tradition, had laid a groundwork of self-loathing. Not to mention my people-pleasing, my fear of failure, my perfectionism, my over-functioning and unsustainable ways of being that had landed me in therapy in the first place. Behind it all was this insidious message that I had to get everything right *all the time*. All the fucking time. Imagine.

That day I picked up my journal, and the gold lettering became suddenly offensive to me. Finding my own value and a voice of my own meant I had the freedom and ability to hold my own ground, say "no," and ask myself what *I* wanted. This is shockingly hard when you are not accustomed to it when you have been given no voice and your "no" has been taken away. I mean, almost painfully hard. Using your voice can immediately throw you into a flight-flight-freeze-or-fawn space, getting hijacked by your trigger, not realizing what's going on - unless you've done the all-important work of figuring out and recognizing your stress responses!

I grabbed a classic black Sharpie marker, fresh and oozing with potential.

I drew a huge X across the front of the journal in the shape of a skull and crossbones. Then I wrote, "Not that I have to." at the bottom: It was my way of rebelling against being told, "Get it right." (Check out the photo on my website if you want to see the artifact itself.)

My internal dialog went like this:

I can get my shit together - if I want to. I can get my shit together - if I say so. I can get my shit together - in whatever way I see fit. It doesn't have to be perfect. I don't have to be perfect. I can stay a mess, and even that is okay. To a certain degree, there will always be messy parts of me. I'm human, after all. And I can hold that dichotomy. I am worthy and have value - whether I have my shit together or not. Amen. Hallelujah. Where's the Tylenol?!

Sometimes, self-compassion starts with a spark of defiance & a black marker. *Hoorah.*

I hope at this point on our journey you have begun to have some grace for yourself. You have identified the natural responses your body and brain are giving you as you deal with the stress of liminality. You have begun to break down rigid, binary thought patterns and opened yourself up to more Both/And flexible thinking. You have taken inventory of all of the moving parts in your life, and even mapped some of your more challenging changes. Well done, you!

I mean, *really* - stop and consider what a lot of work you've done to this point. You are doing something extremely gutsy - you are daring to think there is another way of being! You are identifying what doesn't serve you well and are learning what else it might look like. What a beautiful journey you are on. It is the lovely struggle of navigating the path to authenticity.

Applying your senses to self-care

I want you to reward yourself today.

Say, whhaaaaat?!

Hear me out. Even if it is simply extra cream in your coffee, what would it look like for you to give yourself some sort of reward today for the brave work you are doing?

I'm asking you to do this as a first step because I want it to become a regular occurrence for you. Having a sense of self-compassion includes doing nice things for yourself. Period.

It doesn't have to be a food-related reward if that is triggering for you, and it doesn't even have to be anything physical - it can be intrinsic. Your reward can be a quiet moment of meditation or positive self-affirmations.

It also doesn't have to cost money. A bubble bath, a walk by yourself, or a visit with a friend - whatever sparks you - feeds you peace and wellness.

The first key here is getting curious with yourself. Because you no longer ascribe to binary thinking, you have many choices... what brings you joy, and how can you build time and space into your life to learn that?

I completely understand that this can be extremely hard and even emotional for those of us who were raised with no voice. You learned that doing something for yourself was selfish. It might actually feel really naughty to think about things "serving you." That is understandable with the type of programming some of us receive. You might have gone without expressing this part of yourself for so long that it will take some effort and small steps to get back there. That's OK. This is a journey, after all, and journeys take time.

To help you work in that direction, think in terms of your five senses. If you're going to do something nice for yourself today or on any given day, what might it look like to fulfill your senses in lovely ways?

Sight - look at beautiful photos of nature, take a walk in nature, watch a fun movie

Sound - listen to music, talk with a friend, sing

Smell - use essential oils, bake cookies, simmer a pot of cinnamon and orange slices.

Touch - cuddle up with your favorite blanket, pet your cat or dog, wear some comfy clothes.

Taste - eat the cookies you made above, make yourself a really nourishing lunch with the things *you* like (without having to consider if the kids will eat it or not!)

Again, *curiosity is key!*

Get curious with yourself. What do *you* want? What would make *you* feel nice? What is going to revive you and refuel your tank? What serves you?

One way to help us get past the potential hiccup of not being able to love on ourselves well is to think about how we would care for a close friend or a child in distress who is needing some extra love and care.

Of course you would scoop them up and hold them, speak gently in soothing tones, make them comfortable with blankets by the fireplace, bring them nice foods, listen and affirm and acknowledge and empathize. You would want them to feel supported, heard, and protected. You would let them know they are not alone. Okay, great!

So... don't you deserve that response, too? Can you give yourself that same care? Self compassion is how we think of ourselves, self-care is what we *do* for ourselves out of that compassion.

Okay, self. Let's go get a blanket and sit in that comfy chair in the living room.

On the way, let's message the people I was supposed to meet with later this afternoon and cancel because today is a self-care day.

Could we grab a fresh bottle of water on the way? I always feel better when I stay hydrated. We could even grab some of those cookies from last night and mango to cut up later on.

I think a walk with Tim would be nice later, too. Sort out some of these feelings and be heard by another person - connect.

It's okay that I feel this way. I know where this is coming from... old tapes, old messages. My body is trying to care for me and keep me safe.

Let's stand outside for a moment first and just breathe in some fresh air and look at the sky. I'm so fortunate to live in such a beautiful place. The Creator is amazing.

I'm okay. I'm not alone. This is where I am now. I am safe. I have my "no." I'm an adult with a voice, and I can make choices to care for myself.

"Let's go binge another season of Ted Lasso."

This is what a self-care day can look like for me. This is me leaning in and staying present to my feelings - acknowledging them - but also not letting myself be hijacked by them. Being hijacked by my emotions means obsessing over them instead of giving myself all those lovely choices. This is truly an example of some of the gentle, compassionate things I try to speak to myself *because it is how I would speak to another hurting person in need.* Do I not deserve this same tenderness from my own self? I really do. You do, too.

I have value, and you have value. Treating ourselves in this way is neither selfish nor self-centered. It is self-affirming. Selfishness leaves us hollow and aching for more. Self-care and self-compassion feel like a warm, soft blanket on a cold, miserable day and leave us feeling satisfied. It builds us up and replenishes us, eventually putting us back in the game as a stronger player. Self compassion is life-giving.

Your words - Affirmations

Once we accept what is, slow ourselves down, and start *noticing* in order to create boundaries, we begin the practice of saying good things to ourselves. Affirmations.

I will tell you, in all honesty, I used to absolutely cringe at the practice of using affirmations. I thought it felt so fake and was such a creepy, ooey-gooey thing to do.

Until I realized they work.

I remember vividly the first positive affirmation I used as a sort of mantra - a repeated phrase. I started using it, really, as a joke. Tongue in cheek, I would say to myself in an overly-syrupy voice, "I feel good! I feel great! I feel wonderful!" on those crappy mornings, I just struggled to drag myself along. I would say it to myself five times. The oddest thing was... I actually noticed a shift.

The fact of the matter is, the brain will believe what you tell it. And as brain scientists keep reminding us, repetition leads to stronger neural pathways. Positive self-affirmations may feel dorky, but by-golly, they *work*!

My favorite affirmations I use today come from a deck of cards I found on Amazon called "My little bag of sweary affirmations." My two favorites are perched above my desk: "Not loving myself is absolute bullshit." + "I trust myself because I am a total badass."

Different affirmations work well for different people. You really have to find those that work for you - that resonate with the deeper messages you need to hear and maybe weren't told when you were young and needed them. Affirmations can be a powerful practice in reparenting those places within ourselves that need additional compassion and attention.

They don't have to be elaborate, and in fact, simple is sometimes better. Try things like: "I am safe." "I'm okay." "I've got this." "I am loved." "I am worth it." "I have value & voice."

<u>Your Space</u>

The last thing I really want you to do on this part of navigating your path is to create a space for yourself. We all need some sort of space we can call our own. I fully understand this may be challenging, but please carve out some space for yourself, even if it is small.

Ideally, have a desk space where you can journal and a comfortable chair where you can read. If those activities don't float your boat, maybe it looks like a workout space or an artist studio. Maybe it's the kitchen, or even the garage.

Wherever it is, the idea is to put things there that sing to your soul. Create a space that appeals to you and especially you. It should inspire you, it should be alluring to you, it should draw you in - it is your sacred space.

And you can create your own boundaries around who else is allowed in this space, and how your family is to treat you when you are in your space. It is okay to claim space for yourself. You have value.

If there's anything more life-changing than self-compassion, I don't know what it would be. When I was able to lean into self-compassion, it broke the whole world open for me in a new and beautiful way of living. I suddenly connected with the world differently... authentically. It changed my politics, it changed my religion, it changed how I look at the environment, and it especially changed how I engaged other people.

Loving others well starts with acknowledging our own value. When we see and love ourselves well, the most beautiful side effect is that our capacity to see and love others well is exponentially greater. Certainly more than when we were trying to impress and please the same people. It makes me more tolerant, understanding, and accepting of others-even their mistakes. I'm more empathetic. I have more grace for others when I don't expect perfection from myself.

When I bring my accepted, compassionate, authentic self, I am more fit for the relationship.

Takeaways:

Caring for yourself is not naughty... taking time for yourself is not selfish... and resting is not lazy. Your words are powerful - speak them to yourself with gentleness and compassion.

7

BOUNDARIES & YOUR GLORIOUS "YES!"

"What doesn't kill you makes you stronger."
- Nitsche (...and Kelly Clarkson)

My heart was pounding. I was desperate to make sure no one could see me. I was on the edge of tears and questioning the sanity of the whole mission. Stomach roiling, I hit the button to open the garage door, utterly sure I would pass out from how hard my heart was hammering in my chest.

I was going out to get the mail.

Friend, I want you to know - I get it. At this point in my journey, learning to prioritize myself and actually create healthy boundaries was *terrifying*. Learning to find my voice, as I said before, caused me to make my life very small for a while. During that time, even going out to get the mail, fearing what friendly neighbor I might meet on the street would send me into a tizzy. Truly.

If you find yourself in a place along this journey where, similar to me, you need to take a step back, I encourage you to have massive grace and gentleness with yourself.

Getting curious with yourself and what floats your boat will inevitably lead you to a place where you realize you have some things, and some people, in your life that do not bring the joy and peace you desire during times of transition. Before we talk about the essential need for connection and walking this path with others, let's talk about healthy boundaries.

When we are striving to live up to unachievable measures, we never feel like we are enough and we don't set healthy boundaries for our own self-care because we don't see ourselves as worthy. We will continue to drive ourselves to do more and more, rarely - if ever, saying no. This means we never stop to consider what we want or what we would choose.

What systems in your life serve you and fill you up, giving you energy and life? What activities drain you and strip you of energy? What would you say NO to right now, today, if you weren't thinking about what others might think of you if you stopped?

It is time to slow down. Stop striving. Give yourself time to just be and breathe and listen. Listen to nature, listen to your heartbeat, listen to the rhythms of your surroundings and listen to the creator, the divine, the sacred.

Rest is not lazy. Thank you, Lara Wellman.

When we accept what is, we slow down, and we begin to notice. Love yourself enough to notice what fills you and feeds you, as well as what drains you and exhausts you. When we evaluate what is giving us life, and what is costing us too much, we begin to get an idea of what (even *who*) in our life should be limited or pruned - gently removed. This is what it means to have boundaries.

Boundaries aren't rude or mean. Boundaries are healthy. And they're an essential part of self-compassion. Boundaries say it is okay to remove what no longer serves you. Whatever *it* is. You're making room for what nourishes you. Because you are worth filling your life with good things and good people.

Having boundaries is not *being* a bitch. Not having boundaries... *is* a bitch.

Your Glorious, "Yes!"

I would like to introduce you to your Glorious "Yes!"

When you have done any pruning that needs to happen from your life or calendar, and somebody asks you to do anything more than what you agreed to do, here is a perfect Rule of Life to follow ... Only say "**YES!**" to that which knocks your socks off! I mean, *really* lights your fire! And hear me out, friend. Only say yes when it sounds like this: "***YESSSSSS!!!!***" Only then.

I honestly picture myself in Loki's full green regalia, offering a "glorious" yes because I, too, am burdened with glorious-purpose. Much thanks to Tom Hiddleston for doing a brilliant job bringing that complex character to life in the Marvel Universe.

This idea first scared the absolute crap out of me. Because I also had to practice the "no." I remember the first time I told the nurse at the doctor's office, "No, I don't want to be weighed today." I thought I was going to puke I was shaking so hard. She didn't care one little bit, and we went right on with the appointment as if it was no big deal. But it was HUGE for me!

I have given myself permission to use a couple of key phrases when someone asks something of me. It has been a good stepping stone towards my "no" and buys me some time to consider how glorious my "yes" is! I'll say something like, "Thanks for asking! I'll think about it."

People like the "thanks for asking" part - it makes them feel nice, and I don't have to worry about the fact that I'm about to let them down by not giving them an immediate yes. I've bought myself some time.

Other ways we can create space in conversations to allow ourselves time to create boundaries or even prune things from our lives might include:

"I'll think about it."
"Oh, how fun! What a neat idea." (leave it at that)
"Thanks for thinking of me."
"I just don't have the capacity for that right now, but I appreciate you asking."
"That doesn't work for me."
"That doesn't fit with what I have going on."
"Let me get back to you on that."
"When would you need to know by?"
"Can you send me the details?"

Some of those phrases are harder than others. Sending that follow up message or making the phone call in which you say: "That doesn't work for me" can be difficult until you practice it enough to feel at ease. It really does get easier. I can promise you that.

Notice the absence of an apology in any of those statements. I didn't say, "*I'm sorry*, that doesn't work for me." I might say I'm sorry - if I really am. But I'm

77

not going to say sorry if it is just for their feelings of disappointment. I'm not responsible for their reaction. I'm responsible for finding what brings me life, protecting my boundaries, and offering my YES gloriously.

We can always offer a genuine "Good luck with that!" or "Best wishes on your project!" to soften the blow of no if we feel we need to. We can be truly happy and generous with the other person as we walk away valuing ourselves.

Obviously, there are many variables and sometimes you'll know right away, "That doesn't work for me." And that's okay to say right away, too! It is a matter of growth for most of us who have been groomed to say yes to everything and not to disappoint people.

You have a choice, and you now have a voice.

Please note, the Glorious, "Yes!" is the polar opposite of *shoulding* on yourself. Meaning, when considering what life-giving activities you are going to allow into your schedule, there is not any room for, "Well, I guess I *should*."

This is where you get trapped into owning other people's emotions and living for other people's expectations.

That kind of thinking has no place in an authentic life.

Shed the should, as Becca Claeys would say.

If you particularly identified with the fawning stress response of people pleasing and doing *all the things for all the people*, this might be really hard for you to hear. If so, try some powerful rephrasing.

Instead of, "I *should* go to the group lunch because I went last time, and they'll expect me to be there. Sigh." How about, "I *want* to go to the group lunch because I'm looking forward to connecting with the people there."

If that is not true, however... here is where the need for boundaries comes in. A more appropriate (and true to self - *authentic*) response could look like this: "I don't have the capacity to enjoy that event today, so I won't be going. Hopefully, next time!"

And then don't beat yourself up about it. Find a way to refill your tank instead. (Nap, anyone?)

Many of the things you think you *should* do are focused around care - giving and doing for others - or being concerned with other people's reactions if you don't do the things.

> Volunteering with...
> Teaching that class at...
> Making that meal for...
> Attending the brunch of...
> Going to the party with...

> Being in charge of…
> Running the errand for…
> Signing your kids up for…

These activities are not wrong or bad in and of themselves. It is our motivation that we are looking at here. It is the mindset with which you approach these activities that needs consideration. Are you doing these things because they bring you life and joy, in the midst of all the things you have already going on in life (look back at your liminality inventory if you need a reminder of how much you have going on), or are they things you dread the moment you say yes because you think you *should*?

Again, *should* has no place in an authentic life.

Takeaway:

Boundaries are a self-compassionate tool of curiosity and authentic living, which are essential in liminal times to protect our ability to navigate the challenge as best we can.

8

CIRCLES OF CONNECTION

*"I must be in proximity to people who see the world
differently than me."*
- Ron Ruthruff

Part of the Hero's Journey cycle includes a time when
the Hero is walking through the challenges of the
unknown spaces. That's when mentors and helpers
come alongside to guide and be with them on their
way. It is Sam to Frodo. It is Aslan to Lucy. It is
Gandalf to Bilbo. It is Tink to Peter. It is Keeley to
Rebecca. It is the help of the seer or the sage. Soul
friends. It is the Anam Cara and the Girl Squad. The
Ride or Die allies! There are places for them all on
your journey.

We need genuine connection and companionship
when we are in the struggles of our liminal times. I
was recently speaking to a close friend who is going

through a hard time, and I asked her what makes the easier days better. She surmised that surely it was connection. Feeling she was not alone in the enormity of what was happening in her life.

We all have that need for connection and belonging. We are relational creatures. The felt safety we get from being seen and valued by others is healing and comforting, particularly when we are struggling with heartache or betrayal from some liminal catastrophe that's blindsided us.

There are three essential circles of relationship that need to be engaged for life to be lived at its fullest authenticity and to embrace the opportunities liminality presents us with. We can think of these circles as concentric rings like we see when we toss a pebble into a pond. We start small at the inner circle, and we expand outward to our group and our community. There is value in seeking out a level of interaction with each of these rings.

Inner Circle

The inner circle is a sacred thing. These are the people in your life you can ugly cry in front of. They are the ones who will help you bury the body. Figuratively speaking. They are the ones who you text or call when you don't even have any words - you just know you need someone to see you. You can count on them to be there by your side.

If you already have a small, close-knit circle of friends or even a best friend or two with whom you can share all the deepest, darkest truths of your lived reality with, friends who show you empathy and, help banish shame, you are leaps and bounds ahead of a lot of us. Finding close mates can be harder than finding that perfect pair of jeans or a swimsuit out of season. It can feel like finding hidden treasure.

Here is what I want you to know about this - *it is not just you*. Honestly. People, on the whole, are struggling with their mental health, and relationships are suffering because of it. Of course, they are. All of us are carrying something, and because of that, our capacity for healthy relationships and connection is severely diminished. I no longer resonate with the blanket, bumper-sticker statement: "People suck!" But, perhaps I could get behind the truth of: "People suck at relationships." Yes, *and...* it makes sense. The world is a wild place right now. We are more connected than ever but more vastly alone.

We all need belonging. And it starts with your inner circle. We can endure infinitely more pain in life when we endure it in relationship. This is not only my lived experience, this is absolute fact.

Maybe for you, like me, your inner circle includes your spouse. Maybe you have a sister or a brother-from-another-mother who really, really gets you. If not, I encourage you to put forth the time and energy it takes to develop close relationships. This is not an easy ask, I understand. Engaging relationships take time, and honestly, even more difficult, they take vulnerability. Putting yourself out there can feel like those dreaded days in elementary school when you wondered if anyone would play with you at recess. Yes, there is the potential for rejection. But putting yourself out there also comes with the potential for connection. It is a messy game, this life.

Just like initiating a conversation can feel threatening, putting things on the calendar can seem like the very least important thing when your schedule is so full already. But, I promise you, whatever life you are living now will be enhanced and made richer for the relationships adorning it. Look at the people around you who are already doing the same things you are, or look at the things you are doing and ask yourself who you can invite to do them alongside you. Activity is a wonderful catalyst for developing relationships and getting to know people.

Ages & Stages

Not everyone can be in our inner circle, though, and we all benefit from a variety of different types of relationships in life. We all profit from people who are our same age and at our same stage and also from people who are *not* our age and are in a different stages of life. Engaging in different types of relationships can help us see that there are different purposes for each and that they fulfill different needs for us - and that's okay. Again, not everyone is going to be a BFF.

I have friends I only see once or twice a year, and we really just laugh and hang out at game nights or neighborhood parties. We don't talk about anything deep, and we don't really know about each other's current personal struggles. This type of friendship just offers us a lighthearted escape. This has value when we're struggling through liminal spaces.

I have friends with whom I always do the same activity. What binds us is our common art and our conversations dive deep around that topic, giving us great connection and fulfillment.

I love the friends I have who are a generation, or even two, ahead of me! They just look at things differently than I do! I have an octogenarian neighbor who loves the plants in her yard like I do mine. During a warm summer evening, one might find her wandering around her gorgeous yard in her bathrobe, taking in the flora with a glass of red wine in her hand. She has been known to drop me the most delicious nuggets of wisdom just off the cuff at times like these. Like the time the HOA President was being a busy bee, and she told me, "just don't step into the silence" when she talks. Brilliant. Thanks, Helen. (Helen went boogie boarding in Barbados for her 80th birthday. Helen is my hero.)

There is so much rich value in diversity! Likewise, my younger Millennial friends constantly astound me with their wisdom and candor in how they look at life from a fresh perspective. (*I'm lookin' at you, Rachel.*)

Different people can give us different degrees of interaction, but the goal here is the fulfillment we receive from a life that is connected to others. We hear different perspectives, see different ways of approaching life, and learn other people's stories... And that is a treasure when traversing the liminal plane.

You especially need to find and engage those who are traversing the same liminal planes as you. Others who have lost a child. Others whose spouses are dying. Others who endure military deployments with children to care for daily. Others who are getting divorced. Others who are ill. Others... others... others...

The value of being seen increases exponentially when you are seen by someone who gets it! You know the feeling. When someone else who is there or who has been there understands you. There is something they get about you on a soul level that others (who have not had the same experience) won't get. Those connections are priceless.

Community

The third circle of relationship I believe is essential is your surrounding community. Community can be the area you live in, the group you interact with due to proximity - say, your borough or neighborhood - as well as the groups you seek out and engage with.

There is a richness to life when we plug ourselves into our local community. Joining the YMCA, or local Community Center, seeking out local craft fairs or farmers markets, taking a class, and signing up for book clubs are all ways you can increase your proximity to those who are both like you and different.

We also cannot discount the online community. Many groups of all types exist where you can gather virtually to discuss any hobby or interest. It can be an amazing outlet to the greater world, and I do not discount it or devalue it. Let it be one of your circles.

When learning to tread transition well, we benefit from an expanded view of humanity and diversity in relationships. Get curious about people! An echo chamber does nothing for us. Life is vast, and there is value in engaging people from a variety of lived experiences. This enhances our authenticity. We are richer for it.

We are complex beings with complex needs, and no one type of friend or one relationship can serve to satisfy all the different layers of needs and interests within each of us. But need them, we do.

We thrive in relationship. Caring connection is as vital to your journey as air and water. We need relationship. We need community. And we need to seek it out.

While I hope you see the value of seeking community, I know that some introverts are skimming this section with the utmost aversion - eyes rolling back in their head, toes curled. Too much.

I understand that we may all have different pictures in our heads of what community is, what it looks like, what it *can* look like - all based on what it has looked like in the past for us.

To be clear, community is not necessarily mingling in large groups of strangers. Catch the key word - necessarily. It *can* look like that if that is what excites you and feeds you. But community doesn't *have* to look like that.

For some of us, a volunteer position filling balloons in the back of a hall before the event ever starts, just chatting with the other volunteers and forming relationships in the quiet, pre-party hours is where it's at. And that's great! What I'm saying here is to find community in your own way that suits you. But find it.

Look, I want you to know that what I'm asking you to do is hard. *It is.*

In the lowest times of my journey, I didn't feel like I could bring my dark reality to anyone in my life. That is the Catch-22 nature of feeling lost in liminal spaces - just when we need people the most, we are least likely to reach out to them. I felt those who knew me would have been shocked by the hard details of my experience, and while I was still taking responsibility for other people's reactions, it wasn't an easy option. And it just felt like *so much work.*

Opening yourself up to loving yourself means seeing that you have value to offer others, even when what you bring is a less-than-perfect mess. And others have things to offer you, too. You are not a burden.

Navigating transition with authenticity is best done in the company of others. Truth.

Pruning

When you get curious about the relationships in your life, just like you did with your schedule in creating boundaries, there might need to be some pruning that happens. Sometimes, this looks like deciding certain people or activities shouldn't be in our lives anymore, sometimes, it is just limiting them.

What relationships give you no agency - no choice or voice? Who talks over you or gaslights you into thinking you are crazy for saying or doing something, and makes you doubt yourself, feeling everything is your fault and there must be something wrong with you? Who have you possibly outgrown? Who wants to keep you in the same role you are trying to move out of?

If you came from a dysfunctional family of origin, you might have inadvertently entered into the same kinds of relationships and surrounded yourself with the kinds of people you grew up with. We are comfortable with the familiar. We feel safe with what we know. Even when the familiar is not good for us - and keeps us from our authentic selves and the life we want.

If you have relationships that suck the life from you, step away. You don't have to throw shade, but you can certainly stop and consider your capacity for time spent in that relationship on any given day and say no if it wouldn't serve you well. Bless and release. Internally, thank them for the part they played in your journey, and move on if you need to.

I know this can feel terrifying. Humanity's most basic and desperate fear is the fear of abandonment. Not belonging is dangerous. We can stay safe if we are part of the pack.

When I left my home church of 20 years in the Fall of 2023, I felt like I had culled myself from the herd. I had overridden a very deep need in my brain to belong for safety. I was far enough along in my healing journey, though, that I recognized it was no longer a place I felt safe - I knew leaving was going to offer far more healing than hurt. I have, in fact, moved on from several relationships on this journey. Relationships that relied on a familiar construct of control that became uncomfortable as I gained self-worth and voice.

When you increase your capacity to see your own value, you will be able to walk away from harmful relationships that neither fulfill you nor give you life.

If you continue down the path of self-compassion and trust, the more you will find value in yourself, and the less you will tolerate the meager table scraps unhealthy relationships toss you. Eventually, you will decide you would rather starve than continue to eat their crumbs. And you will walk away.

Just be sure to seek out connection elsewhere, for we are not meant to walk this journey alone. Plus, developing new relationships can soften the blow of releasing some old ones.

. . .

Takeaways:

Navigating the path to authenticity is not done alone. It is not a solo adventure. Belonging enhances us. We need the compassion and connection found in relationship with others.

9

MIND MAPPING YOUR TRANSITIONS

"Here be dragons."

~ Anon

Suddenly, you find yourself in new territory, and the edges of your map are blank. The road ahead fades out to a bare squiggle of a line, and you're left on the threshold of the empty space. This is the place on ancient maps where they would simply draw a monster and a note: Here be dragons.

Can you imagine the explorers peering into their scopes, out into the great blue unknown? The cartographers at their shoulder, asking, *What is it? What do you see?* And the explorers not knowing the answer? That is you on your journey as you approach the reality of liminal life. You are at the edge of the map, and that vague expanse out ahead of you is liminal space, full to the brim of ...the *unknown*.

The unknown can be frightening. More so when you approach it with the rigidity of binary thinking: "There's only *one* way this all comes out right." But there's enchantment in the unknown too. The sense of possibility lures you on.

We are going to map one (or many) of the choices you are faced with right now and all the different ways it *could* go, as well as the different areas of life it affects.

This will not be an exercise of analyzing all the possible outcomes with the goal of getting just the right one.

You are not Marvel's Dr. Stephen Strange, and try as you might, you cannot figure out the one chance that comes out "right" in the middle of 14 million possible outcomes for the Avengers to beat Thanos and achieve victory in the Infinity War. I'm sure some of you could give him a run for his money, though. The over analyzing is strong with this one.

In our house we call it "playing chess." We sit and ruminate on all the possible moves and outcomes of a particular situation. We end up driving ourselves a little batty. Ultimately the goal of this kind of over-thinking is to win, stay safe, avoid pain - and *get it right.*

Instead, the goals of this exploration I am inviting you to participate in are:

- To make room for yourself in your response to your liminality
- To make room for connection to others in your liminal times
- To create healthy boundaries to protect what you have put in place
- To get curious about what serves you

And, ultimately:

- To practice Both/And language when looking at choices, to see that there are many ways that will be okay... experiencing freedom and self-trust in knowing that whatever happens, *you've got this.*

Mapping

Now that you have looked at the liminal places in your life, begun the self-care brought about by getting curious with yourself, and moved toward the opportunity for connection when you get curious with other people, as well as considering all the conversations we've had about boundaries, *shoulding*, and your Glorious "Yes!" - let's put that all together in a practical way. You're going to map some of the challenging choices you face right now to find new creative ways through them. This is where the upgrade happens. You're committed and on your way.

Liminal spaces aren't just for druids anymore. Let's get practical, and discover how you can use your newfound awareness of your stress responses (fight - flight - freeze - fawn) and flexible thinking, coupled with self-care and connection, to make specific adjustments that will result in more authentic living. You've already crossed the threshold portal into your new self, now we begin to navigate.

Maps give us information and guide us on our journey. The invitation in this exploration is to evaluate the impact of the transitions or changes you currently find yourself struggling with, and to purposefully find ways to navigate it with authenticity. This may include:

- Engaging a flexible mindset (how are all the ways this could be "ok")
- Habits of self-compassion (self-care activities and/or places you need healthy boundaries)
- Connecting with Community (where are the places you can draw in support and engage in belonging)

Draw the mind map below, larger, on a blank sheet of paper for each liminal space that is challenging you right now.

- Put the change or transition in the middle. It's ok if this is not a *new* situation, but rather something you find you need help navigating.
- In the boxes, fill in the various *who / what* that will be affected by this change. Add as many as you need to. This is higher level thinking.
- The final ring of smaller circles is *how* those things will be affected & the routines or actions you will need in place for managing that aspect of the change. This is more detailed, specific thinking.

The example scenario I drew out is one in which we imagine what it would be like to be introduced to the liminal space of enduring a chronic illness. You can see that the situation goes in the middle, and the boxes around it are the **who** and **what** affected by the change.

In each of these areas, I have an opportunity to become curious. Not about what I can do to get it right, but rather *what do I want that area to look like? What might bring more life to this situation?* For each area, I want to ask myself: *What do I need and want? What might others need or want from me? What does the situation ask for,* and *What boundaries might I want to put in place?*

Let's take each of the areas of life affected in our example map and look at the choices. Let's see how you might honor yourself and others in those areas of life.

I'm about to get curious... Here's what my internal dialog might sound like:

"The area of finances is going to be a big one... the medical bills are growing and aren't really going anywhere. How could this look? I'm not sure... yet. I might need an advisor. I have seen people willing to help others in this situation, though. That could be an option. In the meantime, we might need to cut back on how many streaming services we have!

Certainly, I'm going to have a learning curve for how to manage my job during this time. But I can do hard things! It's ok to assert myself at work right now and ask for some accommodations. Maybe working from home, maybe adjusting my hours.

This feels like a lot already! I don't think I can manage the house and hold a job - yet! Can I share the responsibilities with others in the house? Can I hire a housekeeper? (Draw a line back to finances.) Could I ask others to bring me meals when my energy is really low? How can I gather community around me to help?

The kids will need after-school care, help with their home-work, and care in general. How do I connect with them in the midst of this shuffle? Could a family time on days I have more energy help? What can I take off the schedule to spend time with them? What might that look like? A lot comes back to that darn schedule... the kids taking the bus will help, for sure.

Relationships are really important to me right now. I've noticed I'm feeling really down about a lot of things. Chronic illness is so depressing. I need to make sure I schedule time for my partner, my family and my friends – even phone calls or texts – to reach out and connect."

Now that all of that information is laid out, pull back up to a 30-thousand foot view and get curious. Consider how all of those aspects of this transition could be navigated with more authenticity by your engagement with self-compassion, flexible mindset and community. Add your thoughts to the three key boxes in the margin of the map. This is your map key.

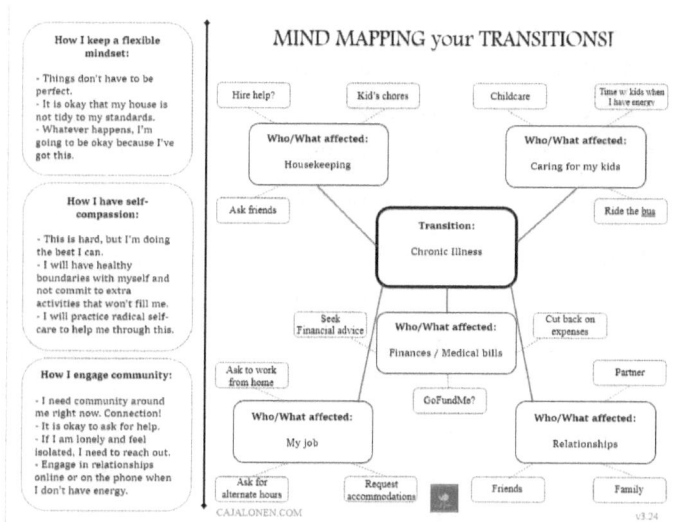

The fact of the matter is most of that processing was questions. I was getting really curious with myself, and I wasn't sure how a lot of it was going to work itself out. There is a lot of open-handed questioning there. I was affirming myself and maintaining flexibility. I was seeking ways to care for myself and engage my relationships. I considered some boundaries when I thought about what I might take off my schedule to make room for things I might prioritize instead. There are even some (?) marks on my map, which is okay - it shows I am staying open to possibilities.

It can be uncomfortable to throw around a lot of questions and not know how things are going to end up. This is the ultimate identity of being in liminal spaces. It is new, and there is so much unknown.

What I encourage you to see, though, is that there are many different ways one scenario can look. We gain *hope* from the fact that we don't have to find just the one right path to achieve peace and success. We can relax a little in the uncertainty.

When we are getting curious with ourselves, we are building a life based on what is best for us and we can rest assured that what results will be authentic living. Authentic living is purposeful, and when we design our choices in such a way that we give ourselves opportunity for curiosity and compassion, what results is living into our best selves.

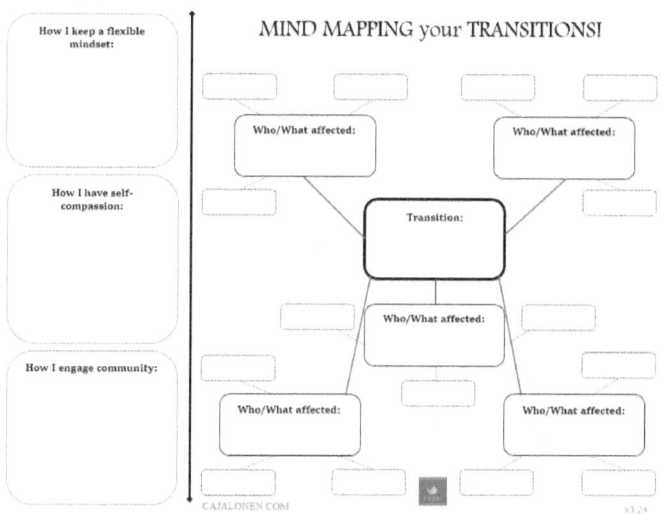

You can get both the blank and sample maps on my website at www.cajalonen.com/mindmappingyour-transitions

Takeaways:

Each liminal space in life is an opportunity to gain authenticity through the compassion and trust it takes to get curious with yourself - what you need from each situation, and what it needs from you. Decide with care what you are willing to offer, and where your boundaries and places of growth are. How can you apply self-compassion, a flexible mindset and draw in community for each transition?

10

BURN THE SHIPS!

"...we answer the call to journey, which is the invitation to transform ourselves by expanding our awareness..."
- Joseph Dispenza

I find myself in an interesting liminal space as I draw near the end of the journey of writing this book. Many of my closest friends are currently enduring the most difficult hardships of their adult lives. They are each in deeply liminal places, taken there by illness, betrayal, and heartache. Their lives are full of confusion and the unknown. As discussed in the liminal inventory chapter, when those close to you are in liminal places, you find yourself there right along with them.

We do life together for this reason. Watching them endure and traverse the rocky path on their own journey has made me really stop to ponder my own points in life when I was brought low, and I started getting curious... What does a Both/And life look like? I mean, *really* look like? Even when we are in the trenches.

Freedom from a binary mindset (the mindset that instills fear and the need to control), changed my outlook on the unknown in my life because, as we have talked about, I now know that there are many outcomes that will be okay because I am okay - I trust myself to be able to handle what comes my way. But there's more than just being okay. And certainly more than being "fine."

I shared with you in Chapter 6 on self-compassion that I gained a completely different world view in almost every area of life since learning to truly value myself and gaining voice and agency: politically, environmentally, relationally, personally and spiritually.

These flipped viewpoints were the key to not only navigating liminal space but just resting in the fullness of life, no matter where I find myself. I got to those new perspectives through a process of slowing down, resting, finding the peace of that space, and then moving forward from that place of renewal. This is what living with authenticity can look like. I now feel called into the gloaming... Liminal life, for me, is not just about navigating anymore, but the opportunity to explore - to get out onto the blank edges of the map and test my limits.

There is beauty when you allow yourself to slow down and stop striving. Authentic living is purposeful living. What is the difference between these two extremes: striving on one hand and purposeful living on the other? *The energy*. Striving comes from a place of "should" and "must" and is focused on boosting your reputation - what others think. Striving doesn't rest. It doesn't slow down when you need a break because it is hardly aware of your needs. Striving pushes forward like the hounds of hell are breathing down your neck. Striving hurts you and hurts those around you through a lack of mindfulness and presence and an energy that pushes.

Purposeful living is what you get when you are your authentic self. Your curiosity for what serves you, your healthy boundaries, and your connectedness - all come from choice. When you have Choice, you are in a place where you can rest in peace and freedom.

When I live in that space of trusting myself and allowing myself to live authentically by being aware of my own agency and leaning into it, I can rest. I am no longer playing mental chess. I am not spending energy (and sleepless nights) trying to figure out the outcomes of all the moving parts in an effort to control what is coming. There are still logistics to figure out in life. I am not suggesting we ignore them. There is a time and place for figuring those things out and then for setting them aside. There is power and freedom in walking away and not allowing your life to be overrun by obsessive thinking.

One really good strategy to manage this when it challenges you is to allow yourself a set time to think about these things. Tell yourself that you have time scheduled to deal with those thoughts, and when it is not that time, those thoughts get put away. Visualize a shelf or a chest in your mind, and see yourself putting those thoughts and all the necessary decisions away until it is time to keep thinking about them again.

Learn to trust yourself by intentionally returning to those thoughts at the designated time. Perhaps even choose a particular place to do this planning and thinking as long as it is not also your comfy relaxing space. Make it a working space. You can process your thoughts about finances, the future, medical decisions - all the things - in this place at this time.

During the rest period, when thoughts come up, gently remind yourself you established a time and place to think about them, and now is not the time or the place. Distract yourself with some self-care and really allow the peace to come. Sit in silence. Practice yoga, Qi Gong, or breathing techniques.

Replace the time you spent worrying with life-giving practices.

When you slow to a stop and rest in that place long enough to live there, you experience an enormously more solid feeling in your own skin. You've gone beyond the shakiness of rigid, fearful living. It is ironic to me that flexibility offers such greater solidity. Flexibility suggests movement, and solidity suggests being sure and unmoving. It is a paradox! How liminal.

When you were a kid, did you ever climb up on that place in the very middle of the teeter-totter and let your legs pump up and down as the other two people rode the board at the opposite ends? That's what this flexible stability feels like to me. I am rock solid in one place as I let the motion carry me in an endless rhythm of motion.

Moving Forward with Manifestation

Speaking of motion, here is where it happens. When we stop striving and slow down enough to rest and really stay there to become solid, we are able to move forward again from a whole new place. For me, that forward motion looks a whole lot like manifestation.

I'll admit, just like with the self-affirmations, manifestation was not at all an idea I used to buy into. However, I sincerely cannot deny the experiences I've had since beginning to live with authenticity.

Manifestation is the idea that things will come to you when you need them to and that you can bring that about through claiming and believing it. Manifestation also usually goes hand-in-hand with the idea that there is a power greater than yourself (different people have different names for it - the universe, God, the sacred, divine, creator, GUS) and that it wants the best for you.

I'm aware that this is a very simple explanation with broad strokes. I'm sure others could enhance the idea with various details and fine points. The fact of the matter is, like many things in life, manifestation looks different to different people - it honestly isn't something I practice on purpose at this point in my life, so I may define it differently in the future. But my point is - as I explore spirituality from a more mystical angle than I was raised with, *I see things I have little explanation for.*

Since I stepped out onto my own path in this way, people and opportunities have

presented themselves with uncanny precision. Even in preparing to write this very chapter, musing over what I might say with just a couple of notes from my editor, I sat to read for my Way of Life: Pilgrimage class at The Seattle School of Theology and Psychology and as I turned the page in Joseph Dispenza's *The Way of the Traveler*, I read the next chapter heading: Spirituality on the Journey. Holy smokes.

Other amazing examples from just this past year include the incredible writing coaches/ editors I found through a happen-chance Facebook search. That I would have found these particular coaches at this specific time in my life is just unexplainable. They are insanely skilled at assisted self-publishing and helping you find your voice and step into your most authentic self.

My incredible art team is another example. They are half a world apart from each other, with me smack dab between them, and love to geek out on liminal spaces just as much as I do!

The writing groups I joined while writing this book are examples of unbelievably safe places where everyone wants the best for everyone else - there is no scarcity mindset, just sharing and joy.

Here is what I know: full authenticity is very honest and very life-giving to self and others. I believe that the powers-that-be honor this when we step out and offer ourselves to the fullness of life. We are here with the spiritual purpose of Being Love, and giving life and love to others (including creatures and creation). I believe this is the "Kingdom of God." The whole system benefits when each of us lives like this. Our success is desired by the Sacred Divine. What a rich realization!

On the Hero's Journey, new perspectives like this become the boon or the elixir. It is the reward you return with so you live differently and offer help to others. These are the signposts along the way that you learn to read with precision because you trust your instincts and intuition. Intuition is your subconscious ability to pick up on and recognize patterns. When we journey through enough of life, turned on to these signs around us, we can more easily read where we are and what is to come - seeing our new way forward.

The forest stays the same - you are still surrounded by trees on the path - just as you are still surrounded by liminal spaces in life. It is *you* who have changed. Instead of the dim light of the gloaming bringing fear of shadows and the unknown, it brings intrigue and adventure. Suddenly, your flexibility has brought solidarity - more certainty than your grasping for control ever did.

Without glorifying the Spanish colonization of Mexico, there was a poignant moment in history when Cortez ordered his men to, "Burn the ships!" He was so determined to move on and not go back, he removed even the option of returning.

When we find ourselves at the end of one path of self-discovery, we realize we can never go back to who or where we were before. We're transformed.

We cannot unsee what we witnessed. We are awake in a way we've never been before. Sometimes, this causes further liminality, giving us an uncomfortable new place to navigate. Like a flower turning toward the sun, our mind will always seek safety. The mind will choose the comfort of what is known. I encourage you to *lead* your mind in this matter. It's opposite to the idea of following your heart. Lead it. Mentally burn the ships, knowing you are changed and cannot go back. Press onward.

Burn the ships!

Takeaways:

You are changing, and that brings with it some discomfort. Allow yourself time to stretch into this new posture, this new way of being. Be gentle with yourself, but resist the urge to go back to what was not serving you.

11

CONCLUSION - LIMINALITY AS LAUNCHING POINT

"A threshold is a sacred thing."
– Esther de Waal

At the beginning of the book, I started telling you a story of a time I took myself out of my norms and comfort zone to snuggle up to that which was different at a Rewilding Retreat on Whidbey Island.

I felt like Bilbo running out the front door of his hobbit hole, yelling, *"I'm going on an adventure!"* I was stepping out. Being brave. I was taking myself into a liminal space, purposefully. Shiver me, timbers.

At the retreat, we went around the council circle telling about ourselves - where and what we were from. *"What"* were we from? That was new for me, too. It refers to being from more than just a geographical place but also from the very nature of that place and our own ancestry as well. It is a holistic way to view the classic question, "Where are you from?" I had definitely achieved my goal of placing myself in the unfamiliar. These women shared, with utter vulnerability, their hearts for the Earth and their relationship with Her.

Daniella cried for the kind of world she feared her 8-year-old son would grow up in. Beka mourned what was happening with the watersheds north of Seattle. Patricia simply sang us her introduction as a way to grieve the mangled deer she had cleared off the road just before arriving. Molly shared her desire to embrace the elder stage of life she found herself in and to share her hard-learned wisdom with others and younger generations, identifying clearly as The Crone. Another woman expressed her rage at what was happening ecologically all around us, and there was much grief, and many tears shed all around the circle over the loss of the Western Red Cedar, vanishing at an alarming rate due to back-to-back drought years and rapid climate change.

As the day went along, we experimented with various exercises and activities to engage our identity and connect with the beautiful place we found ourselves in. We walked through the Heritage Woods - full of old fir, hemlock, and cedar trees drooping their branches to a messy undergrowth of fallen logs and ferns. Huge mushrooms pufffed out in horizontal platforms wherever they could. We stopped five times - once for each of our five senses. The goal was to stop and really hone in on each particular sensory experience. Our eyes took in the greenish-filtered sunlight and rich colors - every variation of green you could imagine. Our ears heard the tree swallows and chickadees pleased by our arrival and occasionally ravens that sounded completely irked. We touched and smelled the plants along the slick, muddy path - but not the prickly ones. Many stopped to listen to the very river rocks along the way. And trees as well - some stepping out to hug the behemoths. Legit.

When it came to taste, thankfully, we stopped in a patch of Salmon berries. When we realized there weren't enough orange-pink berries to go around, some simply reached up and pulled down bright green branches with fresh new buds at the end and nibbled on them! What availability, presence, and willingness to experience life these women displayed.

Although it was clear to me I hadn't yet been awakened to some of the same passions these women held, it was also apparent that they knew something of the world that I didn't yet.

As much as I felt uncomfortable with some of what I experienced that day - drumming, chanting, nature walks - I also felt admiration. Many of these kind souls were further along the path than I was. The path that embraces all things liminal and marches to the beat of your own council drum.

That afternoon, I had my own mini adventure.

Around lunch time I was on sensory overload. I was experiencing a faint or flop response. I felt myself shutting down. For me, it presents as suddenly feeling inordinately sleepy and foggy-headed. I am unable to listen to what is being said to me or process it with clarity, much less respond. I lose words. I stare off into the distance with unfocused eyes.

I approached Mary and shared my status with her: "Just saturated... Good, but full." I needed to step away. She honored this and asked how she could support me.

"Don't lose track of me!"

Being in the woods is not really my comfort zone. Yet. She gently commended me for listening to my body and released me for some quiet time.

It was going to take about 45 minutes to hike back to the lodge from where we were. Heading out to the lunch spot, the group had made their way along a series of woodland footpaths, sometimes only 12 inches wide, across a ravine, up and down some hills. I would bypass that route by taking the service road up and around, skirting the edge of the property. Walking a 10-foot-wide dirt road was much more my jam than trying to make my way back through the labyrinth of paths we had traversed as a group.

Let me tell you - I had never been alone in the woods before!! ACK!

I felt very brave and... crazy-stupid at the same time.

Both/And.

I kept hearing scuttling and scurrying through the undergrowth of sword ferns and huckleberry bushes. I didn't know what the sounds were, but it was likely just the common yellowthroats or marsh wren that lived on the island. Small birds can make a startling amount of ruckus in a bush! Especially when between the sudden, small bush-quakes it was remarkably still and silent. Just the shooshing sound of the wind at the tops of the trees. I just wasn't familiar enough with that ecosystem at the time. I can't even recall how many times I stopped and looked behind me. I was *so* uncomfortable.

But this is what I had brought myself here for. Exposure. Proximity. New experiences. Learning. Liminality.

And hopefully not dying alone in the woods due to some irrational situation I cannot even put words to that haunted my steps all along the way. (I have a long way to go in making peace with the natural world and feeling a part of it.)

During my experience at the Whidbey Institute, I was flexing my liminal muscles. I had to use many tools in my bag.

I recognized my stress responses I described to you earlier & had compassion for myself when I reached my limit. I created a boundary to care for myself. I stepped away, alone, when I became saturated and returned to the group refreshed and more present with those around me.

I engaged in flexible thinking to be able to hear what the women's personal experiences were without judgment. I held space to show empathy for those around me and engaged in beautiful community. It was a humbling experience to be in such an authentic group of people.

Did it make that liminal experience 100% comfortable? No!

But, what it did was allow me to walk through that day and stay in those spaces in a way that was more true to myself. Authentic living.

This was my first purposeful venture into choosing a liminal space for the betterment of myself. Because liminal spaces can absolutely be that. They can better us. They can be launching points to an improved way of being and thinking and seeing, and knowing. They open us to curiosity, perspective, and opportunity.

In fact, every liminal place *could* be this for us. If that is what we ask of it. If that is what we expect of it. We can step into the new territory with expectation and certainty that we will be guided. It's a mindset. It is a shift. We start looking at the uncomfortable places of life differently. And you can do that now. There is an inescapable sight you've been given that you won't be able to un-see the different way life could look.

This journey will not always be easy, and sometimes even the *right* choices do not result in our feeling comfortable. In many ways, I'm not where I want to be *yet*, but I am certainly not where I used to be. I feel absolute gratitude for that insight. I'm grateful that I no longer drag around the idea that one day I will get it all right and suddenly *arrive*, somehow transforming instantly into my most gracious and loving self. Even if I make mistakes or new adventures turn out less than ideal, I know I can still grow from that place, and everything that comes my way serves to make me into a more complex and deep being. I'm so, so okay with that! I get to experience it all liminally - no longer waiting to become the person I wanted to be, or even the life I wanted to have, to arrive.

I hope you can also relate with this feeling. You are not who you were at the beginning of our journey together either. Let's take a look at what we have explored together and remember the lessons we have learned.

We **Prepared Your Path**, showing you how your brain works to keep you safe. When you combined that knowledge with the understanding that binary thinking instigates fear, you gained a powerful insight into your responses to liminal spaces. Then you discovered the key to flexibility with Both/And thinking.

You then took time to do some really personal exploration in **Charting Your Path**. You completed an inventory of all of these moving parts, considered your stress responses, and whether or not you might be holding on to some rigid thinking around those places in your life.

Finally, in **Navigating Your Path**, you became curious with yourself and others. No longer adhering to binary thinking, you realized how many choices you have. You considered what brings you life and what drains you. You looked at what connections you will seek out and where you will find belonging.

At the end of **Navigating Your Path**, you explored the specific things challenging you right now! You reflected on your natural stress responses, and practiced Both/And language while making space for both self-care and connection. Ultimately, you saw that many different outcomes could benefit you. Many can potentially bring peace and/or growth. You increased your trust in yourself by knowing you've got your own back, no matter what happens during your times of transition and change!

You now know how to navigate the liminal spaces in life so you can embrace a **Both/And** mindset gain choice through curiosity, which results in living your most authentic life right now. No longer waiting for the moment to arrive when you feel ready, get it right, or *arrive*. Life is liminal.

At the end of the Hero's Journey cycle, the Hero returns to their life as a changed person. They are resurrected, transformed, and have been renewed. They are not the same people they were when they left. You are no longer who you were at the beginning of this journey. Each liminal journey you are on carries you to a new understanding and experience of yourself and your personal power.

Heroes return with gifts. They're not only changed; they bring new understanding and treasure to share with others. Now, the Hero has the freedom, power, and flexibility to live the life they want from their authentic, core self.

You *can* do this. You *are* doing this! You've got this. You are your own Hero.

I encourage you to have grace for your pace.

Every living thing was birthed from darkness. A seed, frozen in the ground. You, in your mother's womb. The world, at the beginning of time. And this new life transforming within you, revealing your most true and authentic self.

Learning new ways of being takes time and practice. We must be gentle and compassionate with ourselves. We can stop trying to fix it and get it right and instead explore what life has to offer.

Seeing liminality as a potent time of opportunity does not remove the discomfort that goes along with these times of transition or make them completely enjoyable experiences. What it does is increase our capacity to endure the dissonance, the grit to run the race well, and the vision to nurture our quality of life in the middle of the mystery of it all.

When we live in a more authentic way, true to ourselves we really reveal our core self. There is a gentleness, joy, and peace that comes when we accept ourselves. It's time to honor the reality of who we are, where we are in life, and how we handle it.

When we rest into the freedom and flexibility of not knowing and not needing to control, we find peace. There is even more energy and strength available to us when we connect with others on the journey. There is a wholeness and authenticity to life when all of these parts and pieces fit into place.

Authenticity is about knowing yourself, what you want, and living in your power. Be aware of what brings you life and what drains your energy, and structure your life accordingly. Embrace the peace and freedom found in the unexpected, in between spaces.

This is the benediction I leave you with as you continue along your journey and traverse places of liminality in your life…

May you be gentle and curious with yourself, honoring of who you are.

May you find peace and rest, reveling in the freedom from binary thinking.

May you be filled with the intoxicating energy of relationship.

May you live authentically, true to yourself.

May you live in wholeness.

Be well on your journey, Hero…

12

A BLESSING FOR LIVING BETWEEN

~ Kate Bowler

a blessing for living between.

Between miracles.
Between answers.
Between formulas.

Blessed are you who live here,
this space between
simple categories and easy answers.

You who wonder why this is your life,
why you got this diagnosis,
or why you still struggle with infertility,
or why you haven't found your birth parents,
or why you can't kick the addiction
or why your kids haven't come home.

Blessed are you who
build a home on uneasy ground,
who, despite your trying,
your asking, you're searching,
haven't found the satisfying
feeling of discovery.

And blessed are you who never will.
This is not an easy place to live.
Outside of certainty,
outside of knowing,
outside of the truth.

But blessed are you
who realize that love and beauty
and courage and meaning live here too.
Amid the unease and the frustration
and the sleepless nights.
In the way love and courage
show up through people,
through presence, through laughter.

May you be surprised by
your capacity for ambiguity,
for the way it makes you
a great listener and a good friend,
for you are someone who knows
how to feel your way around
in the dark and squint for the stars.

I wish it were easier, dear one.
I wish I could hand you
the answers you seek.

But for now,
may you find comfort
in the fact that you are not alone.
We are all learning to live
in the uncertainty in the unknowing.
So blessed are we who live here together.

ACKNOWLEDGMENTS

Many thanks has to go to my husband and best friend, Tim, first and foremost because he is, and has always been, my biggest cheerleader. You have always told me to dream big and believed I could do whatever it was I put my mind to and do it well. You have matched me step-for-step along this journey and allowed our lives to change because of it. Thank you for building something beautiful with me. I cannot wait to put your books on the shelf alongside mine.

Heartfelt thanks to my kids - Alex, Isaac and Emily. You are my great encouragers. Your play, your deep talks, and your love are a shining light in my life. You are each a gift. I hope I have put something out into the world that not only makes you proud of me, but that will help you each along your own hero's journey.

It is true what they say – writing a book is like experiencing labor and birth. It uses endurance and strength, hoping for that good thing that awaits at the end of the ordeal. And it takes a whole team of midwives to help you bring it into the world and nurses alongside you to check on you and keep you well.

In that light, I have a special thanks to my coaches and editors, Darlene Turriff and Nicole Washburn, in helping midwife this book into the world. Your juicy questions and constantly authentic engagement made all the difference. And to my fellow writers in the Author's Collaborative – you are my sweet nurses, helping to keep me well with your connection and community. Enormous thanks to my dear friend, Deanna, who resonates on the same frequency I do; as well as Becca, Laura, Doreen, Maria, Lara, Dana, Sarah, Laurel, Robin & Robin... *how fortunate are we?!?*

To Jacob Nordby & crew at A Writing Room Collective, thank you for creating a safe space to share my voice and be a writer. Thank you for the community you've created and the vision you have welcomed us all in on. Much love to my precious Wednesday morning silent writing group - such a loving, supportive space.

To my brilliant and talented artists, Rob Williams and Mel Rosado, what fun and energy and beauty you brought to this project! It was a gift to find such kindred souls to collaborate with. I feel like I made new friends. Such a gift.

What a treasure trove of friends I have had alongside me on this journey...

Stephenie H, *Thank you for always being the one person I could rely on to help me hide the body. You are a generous and stalwart best friend.*

Lisa C, *Thank you for giving me a safe place to open my eyes.*

Jen B, *Thank you for being a relentless warrior of an encourager.*

Vera, *Thank you for being my celestial sister across time and space, connected mystically.*

Anna, *Thank you for being a wonderfully safe space to land and share my writing and the writing journey... your email companionship throughout this process has been a blessing.*

AUTHOR'S NOTE

I have used references throughout my book that nod toward Joseph Campbell's Hero's Journey. The Hero's Journey is an archetypal example for self-discovery and speaking through this lens provides a directional tool for gaining agency and providing a sense of identity. Campbell's work, paired with Phil Cousineau's Art of Pilgrimage, Maureen Murdock's Heroine's Journey and Sharon Blackie's If Women Rose Rooted, are all helpful in identifying where we are at on our own journey, what dragon's we might be wrestling, who around us might be helpful companions, and how we are returning changed.

LET'S CONNECT

 CA Jalonen writes with the goal of igniting curiosity and prompting conversations around self-discovery and how we can each see the world differently. She thrives in places where she can deep-dive into meaningful conversations with others, gaining a variety of new perspectives.

Her former careers in Public Relations, Teaching, and Trauma Training have all positioned her perfectly to share her lived experience through her writing.

CA lives a creative life in the Pacific Northwest where she writes from her home on a hill above the Hood Canal. Her great loves are her husband of nearly 30 years, their two adult sons, and pre-teen daughter.

When not writing, you will find CA most likely reading, gardening, cooking with a glass of wine in her hand or playing RPG fantasy video games.

Join the Liminal Life Book Community on Facebook to engage and connect with others also navigating their transitions with authenticity!

Stay connected with her upcoming projects at
www.cajalonen.com

www.ingramcontent.com/pod-product-compliance
Lightning Source LLC
Chambersburg PA
CBHW020356130626
46549CB00006B/2303